Watercolor
Landscape Quilts

Cathy Geier

kp **krause publications**
An Imprint of F+W Publications

700 East State Street • Iola, WI 54990-0001
715-445-2214 • 888-457-2873

Our toll-free number to place an order or obtain
a free catalog is (800) 258-0929.

Library of Congress Catalog Number: 2006928707

ISBN-13: 978-0-89689-272-9
ISBN-10: 0-89689-272-7

Edited by Jessica Demovsky
Designed by Emily Adler

Printed in China

Acknowledgments

I'd like to thank my husband, Ted, for all his help and support while writing this book. From doing extra chores around the house to lending me his artistic eye, from planning meals and doing grocery store runs to sacrificing family vacations, I just want to say, "Honey, I couldn't have done it without you!" To Mom and Dad, for years you have supported my quilting habit with machines, a sewing table, fabrics, and tons of verbal encouragement; what wonderful parents you are! For many years now, the dust bunnies and the dog hairs have been having babies on our floors while I've been playing with little piles of fabrics. Thank you, dear family, for not only putting up with this, but for encouraging me to go for it. Teddy, Elizabeth and Peter, this book is dedicated to you; may you have the same opportunity to follow your dreams.

This is my Father's world, and to my listening ears
All nature sings and round me rings the music of the spheres.
This is my Father's world: I rest me in the thought
Of rocks and trees, of skies and seas
His hand the wonders wrought.
This is my Father's world. O let me ne'er forget
That though the wrong seems oft so strong, God is the ruler yet.
This is my Father's world: why should my heart be sad?
The Lord is King; let the heavens ring!
God reigns; let the earth be glad!
Maltbie D. Babcock

Many, many thanks to Tasha from Michael Miller Fabrics, to Lissa from United Notions/Moda Fabrics, and to Patti from Northcott Silk for getting their beautiful new fabrics to me!

Thanks also to Larry Carver, Terry Donnelly, QT Luong and James Randklev for their generosity in granting copyright permissions. Gentlemen, your photographs are continual sources of amazement and inspiration.

To Jacque, Twyla, and Elizabeth: Though we live thousands of miles apart, thank you for being there for me throughout the years. What a time we shall have when we see *everything* face-to-face! To Connie, thanks for toting my kids around, for feeding one in particular, for watching over them when I am gone, and for testing your delicious recipes on us all. How you have pampered my family!

I also wish to thank my editors for editing, organizing and pulling together all the facets of this book.

Table of Contents

6 Introduction

8 Chapter 1: Inspiration and Design
10 Inspiration
10 Use of a Photograph
12 Mapping a Landscape
16 Establishing Depth
18 Focal Points
19 Balance and Variety
    19 Mountains
    20 Trees and Forests
    21 Lakes
21 Conclusion

22 Chapter 2: Fabrics
24 Fabrics for Colorwash
    25 Painterly Quilts
    26 Pictorial Quilts
28 Creating Depth Through Fabric Choices
29 Scenic Landscape Fabric
    29 Fabrics for Mountains and Distant Hills
    30 Fabrics for Forests and Trees
    33 Fabrics for Foregrounds
34 Fabrics for Painterly Quilts
35 Fabrics for Appliqué

36 Chapter 3: Sewing Construction
38 Supplies
39 Design Wall
40 Drawing Sewing Lines
42 Working With Fabric Squares
43 Piecing Triangles and Rectangles
48 Sewing Perfect Rows
49 Pressing Needs
51 Large Quilts

52 Chapter 4: Putting It All Together

54 Adding Appliqué
55 Special Effects
55 Markers and Pencils
56 Layering Tulle
57 Adding Borders
58 Fuse-Basting
59 Adding Machine Embroidery
60 Quilting
61 Blocking

62 Projects

64 Garden Window
67 Fence Post
70 Daffodil Meadow
73 Covenant Cross
77 A Lake Superior Maple
81 Barn Doors
85 St. Mary Aspen
90 Spring's Call
94 Autumn Triptych
98 River Park with Birches
102 Terrace by the Sea
109 Sedona Red Rocks
113 A Room With a View
121 Victorian Garden Arch

127 Resources

128 About the Author

View from the Forest, 39" x 49". Displayed in a private collection.

Introduction

If you think chocolate is addictive, just wait until you start making these simple landscape quilts. Yes, simple; in many cases the patterns require fewer than five to 10 fabrics! Not only that, but I've developed an easy piecing method using a tear-away foundation to sew all those squares together. Simply speaking, you'll be using a stabilizer as a foundation for your fabric squares, gluing your squares to this foundation, folding along the drafted grid lines, sewing ¼" from the folds and tearing away your foundation. You won't even have to cut your squares perfectly, and the piecing is a snap! When it's done, the quilt top will be totally accurate and effectively stabilized for broderie perse appliqué or machine embroidery.

"Broderie perse?" You might ask, "What is that?" It's just a fancy word for cutting out portions of one printed fabric and appliquéing them to another one. It's the old cut-and-paste from kindergarten; what could be more fun? The appliqués provide an instant focal point, and there are so many gorgeous floral and leaf fabrics on the market now that you can turn out a masterpiece with little effort. There is one other major advantage to broderie perse appliqué: you can hide your mistakes. You don't like the way a couple of sewn squares look? No problem; that's the perfect spot for a leaf or flower!

Have you ever been filled with awe and deep appreciation for the beauty of a particular place? Perhaps you have been fortunate enough to visit some of our national parks and forests and would like to capture a memory like I did in my quilt, View from the Forest. The beauty of a meadow beneath towering peaks, the quiet peace of a forest path, or the exhilaration of standing under a rich red canopy of autumn leaves can all be expressed in landscape quilts. Though the quilts may seem magically created, there are simple ways to achieve their beauty. My goal for this book is to help you put feet on your inspirations so they can take you to the place where special quilts are made.

We will start with the design process. In the following pages I'll show you how to sketch workable ideas on graph paper. We will talk about design elements like foreground, background and focal points. See how simple this is? From there, it's off to the fabric stores. There will be plenty of pictures to help you purchase the right fabrics and simple patterns for you to follow.

Using fabric layering techniques, you can add sparkle and luster to your sky and flowing water to your forests. I'll show you how to create dimension with fabric dye markers. Look at my quilt, Alaskan Nights, on page 17; truly, the sky is the limit when it comes to this style of quilting!

Morning Glory, 73" x 53". Machine pieced, hand quilted. Exhibited at American Quilter's Society, Paducah, Ky.,2001.

Chapter 1

Inspiration and Design

Morning Glory incorporates many of the ideas we will discuss in this chapter. As you look at the quilt, pay attention to how your eyes rove over the landscape. They follow the flowers up and into the scene where the morning sunrise glows behind the mountains. From there, you look to the right and stop at the bird on the fence and, following its glance, you are led back into the landscape. Creating an interesting landscape isn't difficult; I'll show you how to set up a good design and adapt photographs to a pattern on graph paper, as well as set up a landscape with the eye of a painter.

Inspiration

Inspiration for a quilt can begin with a piece of fabric that catches your eye in the quilt shop or a memory you have of a special place. It can start with a photograph in a scenic calendar or a walk in the woods. When just the right fabrics come along, voila! A landscape quilt is born.

Visual inspiration is only one of the ways a quilt idea is born. Landscapes can be inspired by stories, poetry or political opinion. The most satisfying quilts come from the heart, as they express personal feelings and closely held beliefs. My quilt, Morning Glory, expresses my love for the mountains and meadows in Grand Teton National Park. It came from my heart, and through my choice of colors, I conveyed the sense of peace and quiet I feel in the shadow of these mighty mountains. Similarly, my quilt Isaiah 51 (page 36) was inspired by a Bible verse:

"The wilderness He will make like Eden
And the desert like the garden of the Lord."

This quilt expresses my personal faith in the transforming power of the Gospel; through the cross of Christ, a desert is changed into a garden. While neither of these quilts was inspired by a particular scene from a particular place, I used the colors and images found in nature to express myself.

Use of a Photograph

Looking at nature and trying to replicate it in fabric can be tricky. Sometimes a photograph is helpful to visualize a scene. As you study the pictures below, notice that they are not dominated by just one or two elements. Often it is helpful to think of landscape design in terms of thirds. One third of your landscape is devoted to the foreground, one third to the middle ground and one third to the background. Let's look at some good springboard photographs and analyze why they would work for our landscape quilts.

©QT Luong, Terra Galleria, French Wildflowers.

QT Luong's photograph of the French coast contains several things to look at for inspiration when you are choosing a photograph. First, there are at least three distinct landscape elements: sky, water and land. These elements can be drafted in squares and triangles, and it is clear where one element begins and another ends. Second, there are wonderful color combinations in the scene; the deep blues of the water provide a lovely backdrop to the wildflowers. There is a wonderful interplay between warm yellow flowers and the cool tones of the rest of the scene. (Flowers in the foreground are easily reproduced through appliqué in our landscape quilt.)

©QT Luong, Redwood National Park.

The middle ground in this scene is established by the tree trunks, the background by the mist in the forest, and the foreground by a lovely blooming rhododendron. As you visualize this quilt in fabric, think tulle for the mist and appliqué for the shrubbery in the foreground. Both of these special effects will be demonstrated in the projects ahead and in Chapter 4.

©QT Luong, Italy.

The structural elements we are looking for are not found in just wild and natural settings. We can make simple buildings with various colored rooftops (see A Room With a View, page 113). Once again, look at the color contrast between the warm tones of the buildings and the cool Mediterranean Sea.

©QT Luong, Rocky Mountain National Park.

There is a special place in my heart for majestic mountain ranges. In this photo, the color combinations of the changing aspen trees, the stormy gray skies and the foreboding mountains signal the onslaught of the harsh winter season. Notice the rise and the fall of the mountain peaks and the sloping of the evergreen midsection. These structural elements can be recreated in squares and triangles.

Mapping a Landscape

To begin creating a landscape pattern, use graph paper with ¼" squares. Begin sketching with a pencil and eraser. Each square on your paper will represent one square in your quilt top; this way you will know exactly where to go and what needs to happen along the way! If you are using a photograph for inspiration, try to mimic on your graph paper pattern the ups, downs and diagonals of the structural elements in the photo. Let me show you how I do this by looking at three examples of quilts I adapted from photos. You can see the photographs, my graph drawings and the finished quilts. Notice how I simplified and slightly adapted each scene into graph drawings? Take a close look at each photo and its accompanying sketch.

©Terry Donnelly, Grand Tetons.

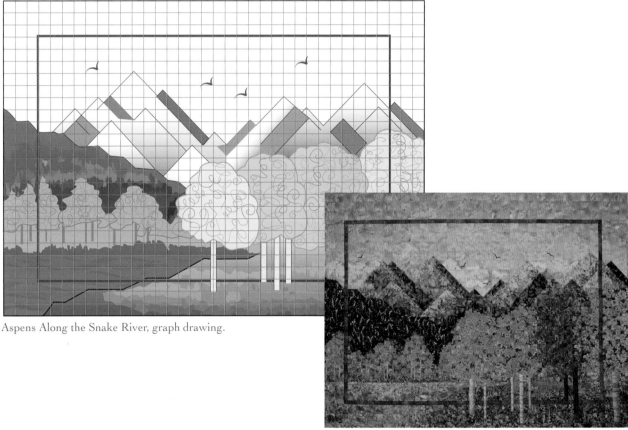

Aspens Along the Snake River, graph drawing.

Aspens Along the Snake River, 59" x 44". Machine pieced, hand and machine quilted. Exhibited at American Quilter's Society, Paducah, Ky. 2003.

Study my graph drawing; the pattern mimics the rock lines found in the photograph. Do you see how these rock formations were simplified? The stone structures in the middle ground are clarified and enlarged. The view through the little arch in the distance is exaggerated. The quilt is as dramatic as the photograph, because I kept the view as seen through Turret Arch and added deep shades of plum corduroy fabric to enhance the shadows. Notice the striped fabrics in the upper-left corner? These add visual interest and texture to this part of the quilt.

©Larry Carver, Turret Arch and Moon.

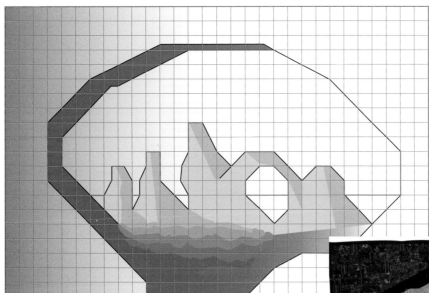

Stone Arches, graph drawing.

Stone Arches, 51" x 38". Machine pieced, hand quilted. Displayed in a private collection.

In our final quilt, notice how the canyon walls have been stretched apart in my pattern. Some of them have been enlarged, and all of them are made distinct from each other. To identify each feature, I used color and value by playing red against gold and incorporating dark shadows. The perspective of the quilt is almost from a bird's-eye point of view, as the viewer can look down over the floor and edge of the river. Tapestry fabric was used to capture the mossy feel of the ledge by the waterfall.

The structural quality of these photographs made them usable.

©James Randklev, Havasu Falls.

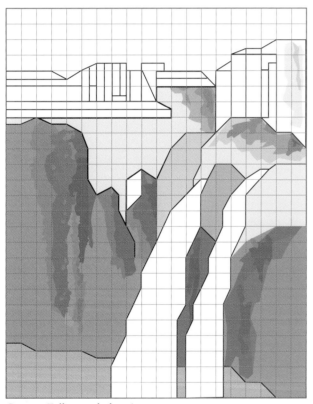

Canyon Falls, graph drawing.

Canyon Falls, 46" x 53". Machine pieced, hand quilted.

Now, take a look at one last photo: the Grand Canyon. Can you see how you could simplify this photograph and make it into a quilt?

©QT Luong, Grand Canyon Temples at Dawn.

This is a trick question; it would be extremely difficult to make a representation of this scene. The subtlety of colors and patterns in the rock would be impossible to catch in fabric with the use of simple squares and triangles. There is neither enough definition and distinction of the structural elements, nor is there more than one element; that would make for a fairly uninteresting quilt top.

As I mentioned before, many times photographs are springboards for ideas. Sometimes, however, it is easier to plan a quilt simply around fabrics you find at the quilt shop. For example, A Lake Superior Maple, on page 77, is not based on an actual scene. Instead, it is meant to convey the wonderful color combinations of changing maple leaves and Virginia creeper against a blue sky and sparkling water. Spring's Call, on page 90, captures a gentle spring day and an invitation to walk; it is not the exact representation of a particular place. Both these landscapes are quilts in which the fabric came first; I liked the fabrics, so I planned a landscape around them.

Establishing Depth

One of the more difficult aspects in these types of quilts is establishing depth. You want to draw the viewer into your scene and make your picture visually interesting. Several years ago, a British comedy troupe developed a sketch poking fun at the British bureaucracy. They set up a phony government department called the Ministry for Putting Things on Top of Other Things. Then, during their TV show, they dressed up as government officials and ran around putting things on top of other things. It was very silly, but I am telling you that the easiest way to establish depth is to put things in front of other things. Put a meadow in front of mountains, a fence in front of the meadow and a tree stump in front of the fence.

Depth can be achieved in two ways: through your colorwash design or through appliqué after the quilt top is sewn. Here are some examples of how to create depth through your colorwash pattern. Notice in all these examples that the richest, darkest fabrics are placed closest to the viewer, and that these values fade into the distance.

Tree of Life, 41½" x 53". Machine pieced, hand quilted. Flowers sprinkle the foreground and lead the eye up and into the tree. The background fades into sunshine.

Midculter Castle, 40½" x 46½". Machine pieced, hand and machine quilted. In the collection of Rose Helmberger. A path draws viewers into the quilt as they follow it down the road and through the castle gate.

There are some very simple ways to create depth using appliqué. If your design doesn't have something to create depth in the foreground, you can use appliqué to push your colorwash design into the background.

Alaskan Nights, 29½" x 24½". Reflections in the water are created with tulle and help further the illusion of distant water and mountains.

Another way to establish depth is by using a fabric's value and scale. We will discuss this more in the next chapter. As you are thinking about ways to build depth into your landscape, you will also need to consider focal points. Simply put: What is going to be interesting in your picture, and how do you lead the viewer's eye to the interesting stuff?

Detail, Isaiah 51. Darker-colored flowers and leaves set the foreground apart from the lighter tones in the middle-ground desert area.

Focal Points

Your landscape should have something that captures the attention of viewers, drawing them into the picture. To illustrate, look at the quilt below. It is a forest with pretty colors, but it lacks interest.

Maples and Aspen with added sapling.

Maples and Aspen, 33" x 38". Machine pieced and quilted.

Now put a sapling in it – see the difference? The finished quilt is much more satisfying.

Your focal point doesn't necessarily need to be one or two things in the foreground. Like our example in Morning Glory, oftentimes the focal point will be the most distant place in your landscape. In View from the Forest on page 6, the focal point is framed by the trees. There is one other thing you need to be aware of as you think focal point: its placement. You will have a much more interesting landscape if you don't place the focal point in the middle of your design!

Spring Forest, 47" x 37". Machine pieced, hand quilted. The middle – where not to place your focal point!

Balance and Variety

Your landscape can be divided into four equal quadrants; simply run a line down the middle vertically and horizontally to see these sections. Ideally, you should have something interesting in each section. As you think about these sections, there are a few things to consider. First, avoid making the scene on the right side exactly like the scene on the left; providing a little variety will make your picture more interesting. Look at Terrace by the Sea on page 102. Notice how the flowers fall down left of center and the birdbath is right of center. These play together by counterbalancing each other. Let's keep these suggestions in mind as we look at some specific landscape elements and how to design and arrange them.

Mountains

There are two important things to think about when you are designing mountains. First, good designs have a variety of peak height and shape. Second, avoid breast-shaped mountains (I bet you didn't think you'd hear about ladies' bosoms in a landscape quilt book!) Take a look at the graphed mountains below.

Notice that all the peaks are the same height and basically the same shape. Also, notice the shapes themselves; this is a particular problem anytime you have just two mountains. While creating your scene, you may not have thought about the shape, but as soon as you do – or a friend laughs about it – you will always regret that you missed it. There are some good designs containing mountain formations on pages 73 and 85.

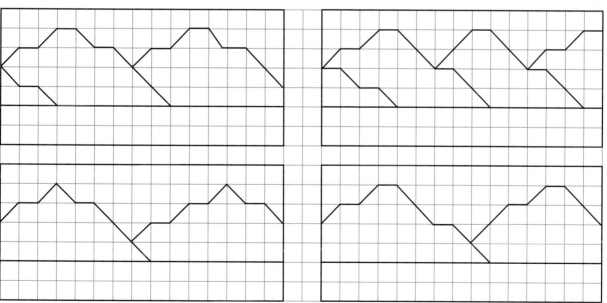
Problematic mountain peaks.

Trees and Forests

When you are creating your trees, angle the triangle portions of the branches and trunks, and adjust their heights and branching patterns. The interplay between two tree branches can make a neat effect.

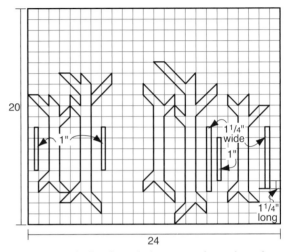

Add variety in the height and placement of your branches.

Detail, View from the Forest.

A variety of branch heights can add interest to the tree canopy. A variety in the trunk-root portion does the same on the forest floor and provides a wonderful place to frame a flower or a leaf. (See Autumn Triptych, page 94). You will need to keep in mind the sizes of the trees you are rendering. The trees in the foreground will be bigger, and their branches will start further up the tree trunks than the trees behind them.

Trees can also be appliquéd to the finished quilt top, adding a touch of realism.

Detail, River Park with Birches.

Lakes

Lakes are easily designed. They can be placed in the middle ground, as in A Lake Superior Maple on page 77, or they can be in the foreground, as in St. Mary's Aspen on page 85. If you are building a lake and a shoreline, try arranging triangular pieces to give the impression of land jutting into the sea. (See Terrace by the Sea, page 102).

Conclusion

Although all of these principles may seem overwhelming, if you study the quilts pictured in this book, you'll see how to incorporate many of these ideas into your own patterns. Not up to creating an original right off the bat? There are a lot of patterns and ideas to get you started in the following pages. Feel free to change and adapt them, perhaps mixing and matching the various elements. Before you dive in, however, let me show you how to choose good fabrics for your projects.

Autumn on the Lake, 56" x 44". Machine pieced, hand quilted. Displayed in the collection of Kate Malloy.

Chapter 2

Fabrics

Here is a quilt inspired by the view of Lake Superior from Pictured Rocks National Lakeshore. Landscapes, unlike other quilts, simply cannot be put together without the right stuff. In this chapter we will talk fabrics, fabrics and more fabrics! Study the pictures carefully; the types of prints you need to shop for are illustrated throughout this chapter.

Fabrics for Colorwash

The best landscapes have the best fabrics. While specific fabrics will come and go, there will always be similar types of certain fabrics on the shelves: leaves, sky fabrics, water fabrics, etc. The patterns in this book are suitable for many different specific prints, depending on what you find available. Before we begin, let me put a word in for your local quilt shop. They have a narrow clientele and are completely dependent on you, the quilter. They will disappear if you don't shop there. Always try to purchase fabrics from your local quilt shop before going online. Now, let's talk fabrics.

There are two different styles in watercolor landscape quilting. The first style is described as painterly; the second is pictorial. Painterly is an art history term for a style in which the beauty of the subject is expressed through the artist's brushwork. When you look at a painterly rendition of a bouquet of flowers, for example, you will notice the artist's individual brushstrokes; you will see that slash of white paint where light is shining on a petal. Pictorial is a term meaning like a photograph. This would imply that the artist is strictly bound by what he sees in front of him. In this case, the artist's brushstrokes would be so smooth that one wouldn't be able to see his hand at work.

Watercolor quilts are typically painterly in nature; the artists use hundreds of different fabrics in their palette. While more is usually better in landscape quilts, the patterns ahead are designed for fewer fabrics. Before you begin creating your landscape, you should decide if you are going for a painterly or pictorial look; these two styles do not blend together easily. While landscape quilts in either of these styles can be gorgeous, there are particular advantages and disadvantages to both.

Painterly Quilts

Autumn on the Lake, pictured on this chapter's opening page, demonstrates the painterly style of landscape construction. It is completely impressionistic in nature. Cut-up yellow and red floral fabrics make up the tree leaves, while cut-up brown prints do the same for the tree trunks; a slew of differing fabrics give the impression of maple trees in the fall. Fabrics can range from small calicos to medium and large multicolor prints. When you are creating a painterly landscape, anything goes!

Detail, Autumn on the Lake. In a painterly quilt, busy prints can even suggest water.

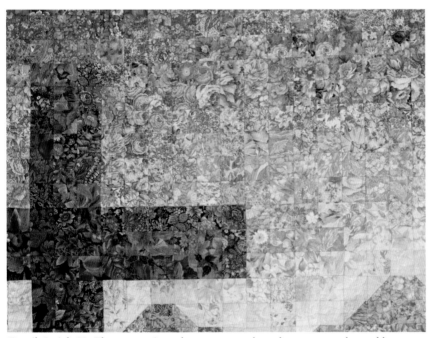

Detail, Isaiah 51. The more prints, the more marvelous the texture, color and beauty.

Painterly landscapes are admired for the wonderful textures and colors that are brought into the quilts when one is free from the realistic fabric constraint. The disadvantage of this style of quilting is that you will need more prints – many prints!

Pictorial Quilts

Fence Post, on page 67, is an example of a pictorial-style quilt; the mountains are gray, the bluffs are green, the sky is blue, etc. One advantage of the pictorial style is that it is easier to build an impression of mountains, lakes and trees if you have used realistic mountain, lake and tree fabric. Often, the pictorial landscape fabrics will be smooth and subtle prints. These blend together easily and provide a nice contrast to the focal point, which will usually be appliquéd. The disadvantage of these types of quilts is that many times, the realistic fabrics lack variety and are hard to find.

General Tips for Fabric Purchases

As you shop, there are a couple of things to think about. The first is the fabric's color value; how dark and rich is the color? The best fabrics have a blend of light and medium values and an irregular print pattern. The second is what the fabric will look like as finished 1¾" squares. For example, in realistic landscape bluffs, I often choose large, mottled-green leaf prints. When they are cut up, those mottled lines suggest topography or hillsides. No matter how you are designing your quilt, avoid any print that reads as a solid color.

The hardest part of landscape quilt creation is determining where one element ends and another begins. There are two ways to solve this problem. One is in your design phase. Instead of blending one mountain range into the distance, create three different ranges and use three different shades of one color to create them. In A Room With a View, on page 113, I used three to four different green fabrics to create the distant hills and spared myself the effort of trying to buy between six and 10 green prints that flowed smoothly into one another. When you're considering your fabric needs for many of the projects, keep in mind that some of them call for fabric scraps; a scrap should be at least 12" x 12".

Detail, Garden Window. Mottled green prints make great hillsides. Each hill is its own fabric; this is an easy way to design hills!

Detail, A Lake Superior Maple.

Another way to solve the blending problem is through appliqué. In A Lake Superior Maple, on page 77, the canopy of a tree meets the sky. The easiest solution is to appliqué portions of the canopy fabric over the sky fabric after the quilt top is stitched together. If this doesn't sound appealing, the other option involves good luck. You'll need to find a fabric that does the work for you, and these are hard to find. For our tree canopy example, you'll need at least two fabrics – one with mostly leaves and a little sky, and one with a lot of sky and few leaves. Appliqué is easier.

The last general tip I have for you is to buy small amounts of many fabrics. I usually buy ¼ yd. pieces; this is enough for most small wall hangings, and if the fabric doesn't work out, I haven't invested much money in a bad choice. If, however, I am certain the fabric is great, I'll buy at least ½ yd.

Creating Depth Through Fabric Choices

As you're building your palette, remember also that you will be using the value of a fabric to create depth in your landscape. Rich, intense colors have darker values and need to be in the foreground. Gray, muted fabrics have lighter values and are best placed in the background.

Wildflowers by the Sea, 29½" x 21½". Lighter prints establish distance.

The other way to establish depth is by the use of scale. A large print will look closer; it needs to be in the foreground. A tiny print will recede. This phenomenon, however, is subject to the power of a fabric's value. Your fabric may be a small print, but if its color is stronger or more intense than the colors around it, it won't recede. Conversely, if a large print is somewhat gray in nature and of a lighter value than the fabrics around it, it will recede into your landscape even though it is a large print.

Detail, Spring's Call. Tiny prints look farther away; conversely, large prints bring the foreground trees up close.

Detail, Maples and Aspen. Small, bold prints are in the foreground, and large, muted prints are in the middle ground.

Scenic Landscape Fabric

One of the best fabric trends to come along in recent years is the scenic landscape print. Whole pictures come ready to cut up and be rearranged into an original work of art. The fabrics are fantastic for use in many different quilts and can be employed almost exclusively in many others. When these bolts come into my local quilt shop, I buy at least two yards. In Spring's Call, on page 90, the path and much of the understory are created from one such print. By appliquéing trees or flowers over a scenic print, your quilt can become truly unique.

The following pages feature thumbnails of fabrics that would be good for our purposes. I have organized them by type, and, as you study the pictures, you will begin to get the idea of what to look for when you are buying fabric for your landscape.

Autumn Oaks and Aspen, 26" x 21". Most of this landscape is from the same fantastic scenic print!

Fabrics for Mountains and Distant Hills

Look at the wrong side of your fabrics as well as the right side. Sometimes the wrong side is just right!

Mountains

Distant Hills

Fabrics for Forests and Trees

Mix together large and small prints of the tree trunk fabrics and tree canopy fabrics for desired look. The forest floor prints also work well in the tree canopy.

Tree Trunks

Tree Canopy
(Mix together large and small prints)

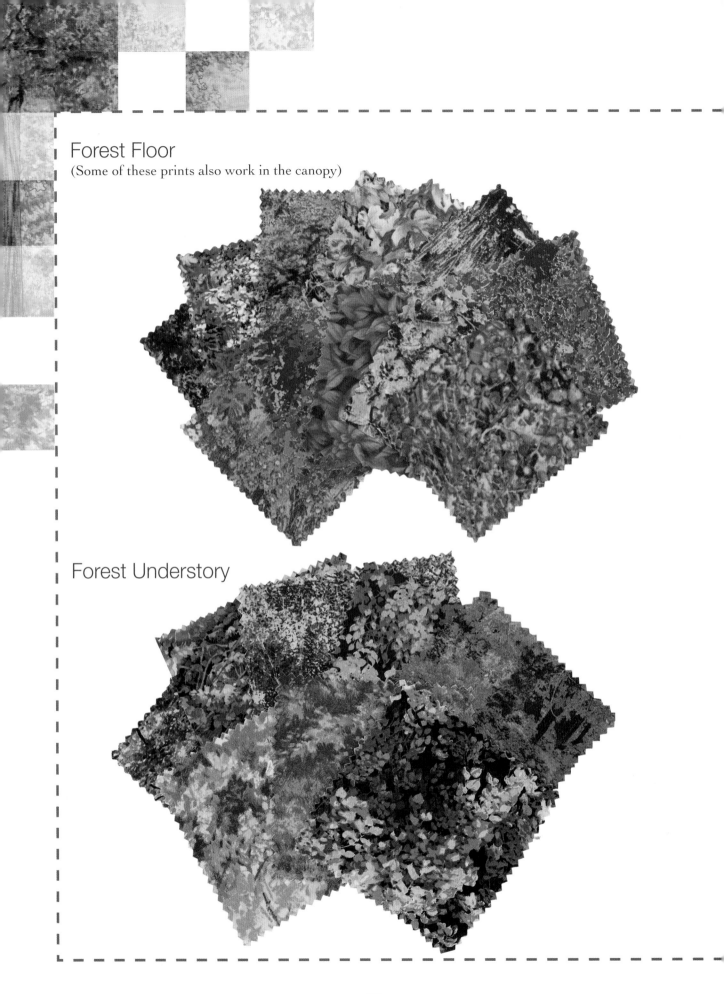

Forest Floor
(Some of these prints also work in the canopy)

Forest Understory

Fabrics for Foregrounds

Usually these are small, busy prints, unless you choose to appliqué cut-out leaves or flowers over a smooth foreground print. The general foreground prints will also work for forest floors. (See A Lake Superior Maple, page 77, or Garden Window, page 64).

General Foreground Prints
(Some of these are also appropriate for forest floors)

Fabrics for Southwest Landscapes

Fabrics for Painterly Quilts

Colorwash Mountains, 36½" x 14½". Many different prints can be used for these landscapes.

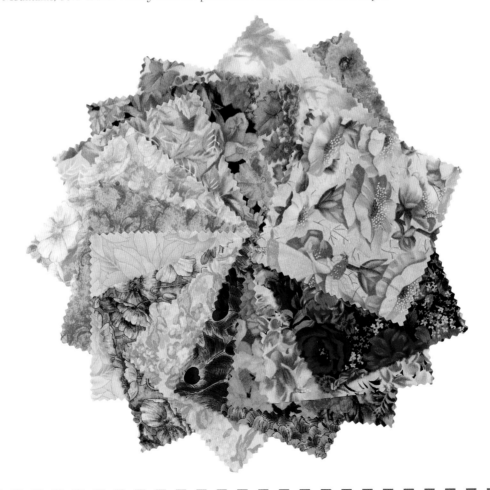

Fabrics for Appliqué

Although any fabric can have pieces cut out and pasted over another fabric, the easiest fabrics to choose for broderie perse appliqué are those that have clear outlines. Flowers, leaves and branches can all be cut out and fused to your quilt top. I especially recommend fabrics that have fine metallic outlines: The metallic line created by the manufacturer lessens the unraveling of the raw edges of the cutouts.

There are times when you will want to cut out an irregular shape of a fabric for one reason or another, whether it's to hide a spot that doesn't blend or to add texture and build up an area in a collage-like fashion. In these cases, it is helpful to think of cutting out smooth irregular jigsaw puzzle shapes. These shapes will be fused on after the quilt top is assembled.

Here are some thumbnails of various types of fabrics to look for when you need an appliqué.

Now that we have discussed fabrics for your landscape quilts, let's get to the actual construction. We will go through the process step by step. But before you start thinking that making one of these quilts entails sewing squares together for the rest of your life, read Chapter 3 about how to use a tear-away foundation to construct the quilt top. It is easier, much faster and more accurate; what more could a quilter want?

Isaiah 51, 72½" x 52½". Machine pieced, hand quilted. Hanging in Living Word Presbyterian Church, Coeur d'Alene, Idaho.

Sewing Construction

Rather like the lyrics in David Mallett's "Garden Song" – "Inch by inch, row by row, gonna make this garden grow" – this quilt took months to piece. I am going to teach you a new method of quilt construction. It combines the ease and speed of fusible quilt grids with the precision and accuracy of paper piecing. Once you've used a tear-away foundation, you'll never sew individual squares together again. This technique can also be used in piecing other types of quilt tops!

There is no doubt that the most tedious aspect of these quilts' construction was the sewing together of all those squares. Not only was it boring and time-consuming, it just wasn't accurate. No matter how careful I was in the cutting and sewing, the fabrics had differing thread counts and those variations in the fabric's stability added up to big headaches in quilt construction.

Here is a better way to put these quilts together: Use a tear-away foundation. With a little time spent in up-front preparation, we will save hours and hours of piecing time. Once the foundation is prepared, we will glue our fabrics to it and then fold and sew along the grid lines we create. When we're done, we'll tear the foundation away. All that will be left is a perfectly pieced quilt top done in half the time the traditional method would require.

Many quilters have asked me over the years why I don't use a fusible stabilizer as a foundation for my watercolor quilts; let me explain my reasons. Fusibles have a bias; therefore, they stretch on one side. To illustrate, if you start with a perfectly square fusible piece containing seven rows of seven squares in each row and construct the quilt top according to directions, you will end up with a rectangle; the square will be off by at least ¼" on one side – and that is working with just seven squares. The larger the piece, the more askew the dimensions. In order to compensate, the quilter has to wet and stretch the patchwork back into a square. This always leads to curved seams. The other problem with fusibles is that they leave bulk in the seam allowances. For every layer of fabric, there will be another layer of a fusible, and that translates to four layers in each seam and eight in the corners.

Picture drafting our graph paper patterns onto a tear-away foundation; once the drafting is done and the fabrics are arranged, we just fold along draft lines, sew along the fold and tear off the foundation. Easy as pie, but without the baggage a fusible brings. Let's get started!

Supplies

- Design wall (see page 39)
- Small sharp scissors
- Tear-away foundation, 21"-22" wide
- Large cutting mat, at least 35"
- Rotary cutter
- Ruler
- Rotary ruler
- Masking tape
- 90/14 universal or topstitch needles
- Sharps 70/10 for appliqué
- Monofilament thread
- Strong thread (neutral colors)
- Acid-free glue sticks for paper projects
- Straight pins
- Ballpoint pens in red and blue or black ink

Supplies

Design Wall

Great quilts are planned on design walls; you need to stand back and view your composition from a vertical angle. You can get a portable wall for under $10 by buying an 8-foot-by-4-foot foam insulation panel from your local building store. They can cut it for you. If you can't get it all in the car, keep as big a piece as you can fit. Cover the panel with batting to hide the markings. The foam panel is lightweight, and you can prop it against the wall and slide it behind a door or couch if you need to put it away somewhere. The panels will droop and slump after a while, so I nailed mine to a wall. If you have space to play, buy two; that way you can create bigger quilts.

Let's get started and create a quilt! Prepare your fabric by pre-washing reds and any strong colors you suspect might bleed.

Determine and cut lengths of foundation required to complete the pattern. Each pattern will give the yardage for the amount of 21-22" foundation that you will need to purchase. The way to lay out the foundation will be illustrated on the patterns with a green line. If you are creating your own pattern and need to determine the amount of foundation required, all you have to do is multiply the number of squares in your grid by the size of your squares and add 1" to that length. Remember that each square on your pattern graph equals one square on your foundation. Any wrinkles in the foundation can be smoothed out easily with a warm iron. Label each section top left, top right, etc.

For our Daffodil Meadow example, we will cut two lengths of foundation, each 28" long (12 squares multiplied by 2¼ plus 1", hence we need two yd. of foundation).

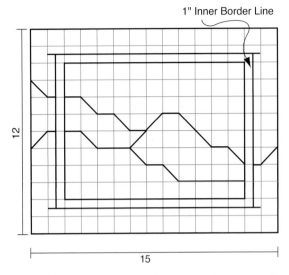

The Daffodil Meadow pattern is 15 squares x 12 squares. We must draft out a grid of 15 squares x 12 squares. Each square will be 2¼" x 2¼". Because our foundation can only hold nine rows of squares, we will need two sections of foundation for this quilt top.

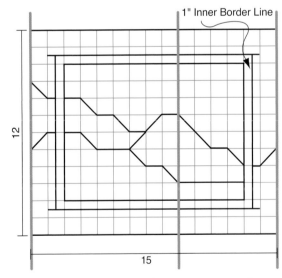

Here is the layout with the green line. It is in two sections; the first section is 9 squares x 12 squares, and the second is 6 squares x 12 squares. Put together, we have 15 squares x 12 squares.

Drawing Sewing Lines

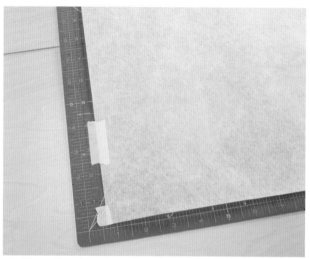

1 Tape Section 1 to one side of your rotary mat, aligning the foundation roughly ¼" over the 1" marking line of your mat. Overlap it on both your vertical and horizontal line.

3 Using your rotary ruler, draw a short grid line every 2¼" across the length of your foundation, keeping your pen point against the edge of your rotary ruler. Use both the measuring lines on the mat and your ruler to ensure accuracy.

2 Using a ball point pen and your rotary ruler, draw the 1" measuring line on your foundation. Line up the edge of your ruler with the measuring lines on the mat, keeping your pen right up against the ruler as you draw the vertical and horizontal lines. These are your plumb lines.

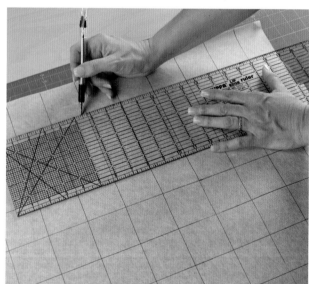

4 Draft your long grid lines in the same way. In some patterns you may have to start from one end of the mat and move the ruler to the other end.

5 Referring to your pattern, draft your diagonals for half-square triangles. Be very precise and draw corner to corner. Add other sewing lines as the pattern calls for them, including inner border rectangles. These lines can be drawn in red ink, if desired.

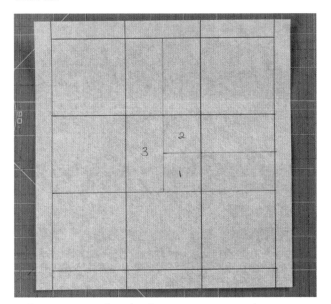

6 Draw inner border lines, measuring the proper width from the grid line according to the pattern. Be sure to follow through the inner border corner squares as illustrated in the patterns.

More complicated patterns will require you to draft very precise scalene triangles within your grid. These sections will be pieced paper-piecing style on the foundation itself. In order to draw these angles in particular squares, you will need to use your rotary ruler and sketch out a ¼" seam allowance inside your grid lines. Then your sewing lines must be drafted from these ¼" seam allowance points and not from the gridlines themselves. Draw these scalene angles well beyond the grid lines as illustrated in the photo below.

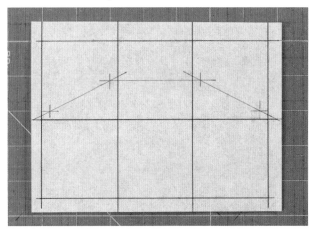

You will need to learn to draft scalene triangles in order to piece all but the easiest patterns. Unless your pattern states otherwise, all scalene triangles should be drawn halfway through your square or 1⅛" from the grid line.

When you are done drawing both your grid and sewing lines on your foundation sections, you are ready to design and create! As you become familiar with this process it won't take you more than 15 minutes to draft out a small wall hanging.

Working with Fabric Squares

1 Cut your fabrics into generous 2⅛" squares. Cutting fabrics a tad smaller than your grid saves trimming time; you don't want any fabric overlapping the grid lines. As a general rule, don't cut up all of your fabric at one time. Instead, just cut a strip or two until you know that particular fabric works. You can cut more as your design progresses.

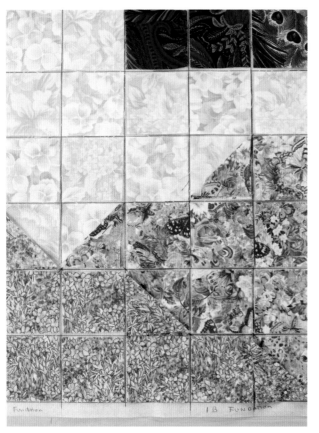

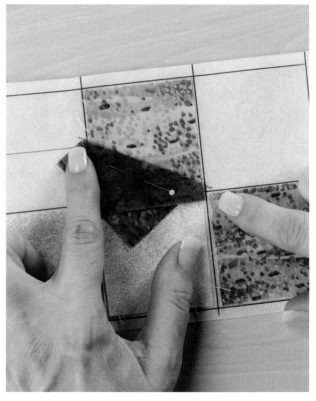

3 Fold the scalene triangles into place as well. Carefully line up the crease with the ends of your draft lines. The fold you create will help you know where to place the fabric when we get to the piecing.

4 When you are happy with your design, use your glue sticks to glue your squares to the foundation. You won't need a lot of glue; just lightly swipe the center of each gridded square and press the fabric to it. It is extremely important that you *do not* get any glue within ¼" of your grid lines where you will be sewing! Removing the foundation can be terribly difficult when it is both glued and sewn into your seams.

2 Arrange your fabrics on your foundation and pin in place, or arrange them on a piece of batting on your design wall. I design on batting because it holds the fabrics and I can avoid pinning each piece as I play. If using your batting, keep rows even and straight as you design. Your fabrics will be transferred to your foundation when you are ready to sew it together.

Piecing Triangles and Rectangles

Piece the half-square triangles, rectangles or any other odd shapes you might have. There are two ways to accomplish this. The first is simply to sew the pieces together and glue them to the foundation, lining up the seams with your drawn lines. This is faster, but less accurate. If you really hate paper piecing, this might be your preferable option! The second way is to sew your pieces directly to your foundation. It takes more time, but it is very accurate. I routinely choose option two. Here are the piecing details:

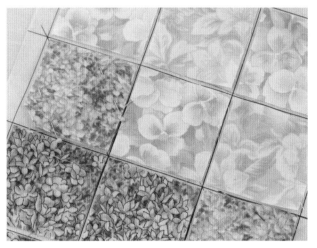

3 Flip the foundation over and sew along the diagonal line using tiny stitches and your large 90/14 needle. In cases where there are many different diagonals, use pins as your guide.

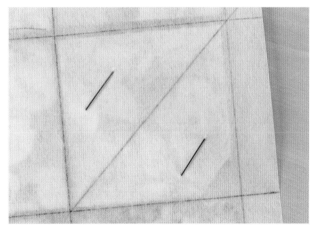

1 **To piece triangles,** begin by snipping off your unused corner. This will prevent mix-ups in orientation when you finish piecing.

2 Lay your fabrics right sides together on the foundation. Make sure that the background fabric is on the bottom and that it fills its portion of the half-square triangle. As you lay your top fabric, make sure that when your diagonal is sewn and the top fabric is folded back into place that the rest of the grid is filled. For example, if your pieced triangle will be folded down and to the left, pin the top fabric square further up and to the right. Pin fabrics to the foundation, keeping pins parallel to the diagonal line you drew.

4 Before beginning each new seam, keep your needle in its down position and lift up your foundation a bit, checking to make sure the fabric has not become folded or bunched up underneath. Sew your seam. Turn your foundation over, open your fabrics and trim excess seam allowances. Glue in place.

1 **To piece rectangles,** position your background fabrics right side up, ¼" over your drawn lines (the red ones in the illustration above). Lay your other fabric on top, right side down, also overlapping the draft line. Pin in place.

When sewing long rows of rectangles, alternate the fabric layout so that when the fold and sew process is complete, these units have opposing seams. This cuts down on excess bulk in the seam allowances.

2 Flip your foundation to the back and sew along your drafting lines, using tiny stitches and your large 90/14 needle. Before beginning each new seam, keep your needle in its down position and lift up your foundation a bit, checking to make sure the fabric has not become folded or bunched up underneath. Sew your seam. Open your rectangles, trim off the excess seam allowance, finger press fully open and glue in place.

1 **To piece scalene triangles,** let's piece a rooftop to illustrate! Start by gluing the background fabric to the foundation, but glue only the portion that will remain on the foundation. Carefully align the crease you made with the scalene draft line. Make sure that when the seam is sewn and the fabric is opened up, it will fill its intended space. Keeping both fabrics in place, open the folded fabric and pin parallel to the sewing line.

2 Flip the foundation to the back and sew in place using tiny stitches. Open and trim off the excess seam allowance. If you prefer, cut larger pieces of your fabric to sew these triangles; that way, the alignment isn't so tricky.

3 Sew along your draft line. Fold back your triangle, finger press it open, trim th excess seam allowance and glue it in place.

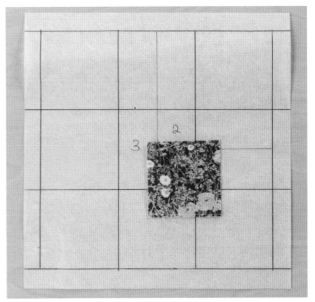

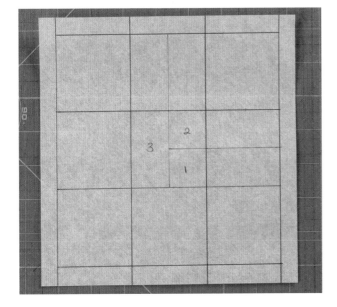

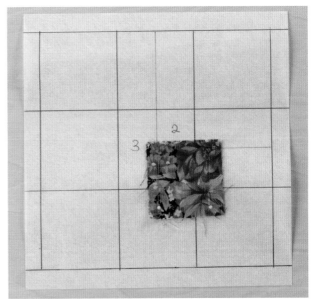

4 Finish the house and rooftop with the scalene triangles.

1 **To sew multiple patches,** determine the piecing order necessary to have all of your seams finished within one square on the grid. It is also important that as you sew and trim the first few patches, you leave enough fabric for seam allowances in subsequent patches.

2 To create an inner border corner glue your background patch ¼" over the draft lines within the grid.

3 Align the second patch over the first. Pin it in place, flip the foundation to the back and sew along the short draft line.

4 Flip the foundation to the front again. Finger press the seam fully open and glue in place. Trim off excess fabric, making sure to leave enough for the next seam allowance.

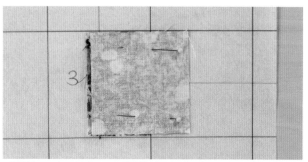

5 Place last piece of fabric over the pieced set, right side down, and pin in place. Once again, flip the foundation to the back and sew along your long draft line. Finger press open, trim and glue remaining patch in place.

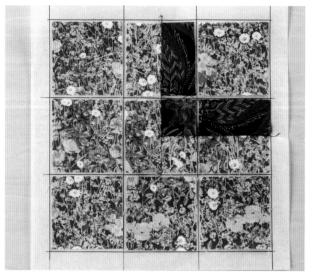

Here is our completed inner border corner.

Let's look at the process with triangles:

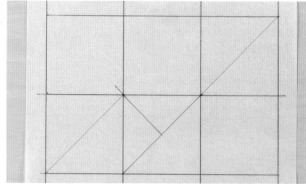

To sew multiple patches with triangles, look at this example of a square requiring three patches.

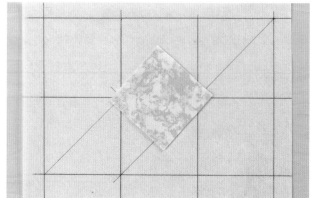

1 Start by gluing your background patch ¼" over the draft lines within the grid. We will pretend this is part of a mountain range with a distant peak and a blue sky. Our background patch will be a sky print.

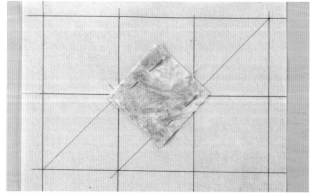

2 Align your second patch, double checking that when it is opened it will fill the second space within the grid. Pin it in place, flip the foundation to the back and sew your short diagonal line.

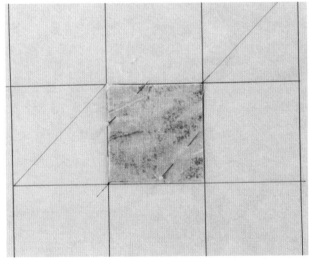

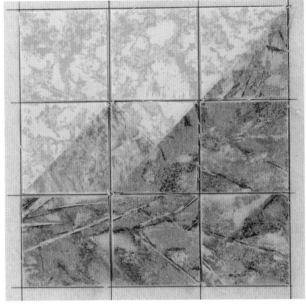

3 Finger press your pieces open and glue the second patch in place. Trim, making sure to leave ¼" over the next seam line.

4 Pin the final piece in place, flip the foundation to the back side and sew the long diagonal. Finger press it open, and glue it in place.

5 Finish additional patches to complete the section.

Many of the more complicated patterns will require a particular order for piecing, which will be illustrated in the project pattern itself. I strongly recommend foundation piecing when it comes to these angles and patches.

Sewing Perfect Rows

1 Finish the entire grid with squares. If your fabrics have become flippy, just press them with a warm iron. Double-check and trim away any fabrics which may overlap the grid line.

2 Fold and sew your rows. Start the process with the rows that are parallel to the seam where the foundation sections will be joined. As in the Daffodil Meadow example on page 39, begin to fold and sew the vertical seams. Fold precisely along each grid line, and sew using tiny, tiny stitches and your large sewing needle! Set your stitch length to barely creep along, at least doubling the number of stitches your sewing machine settings suggest. (My stitches are too small to count.) Remember, you will be tearing along these perforations, so the thicker your foundation, the more holes you need to make.

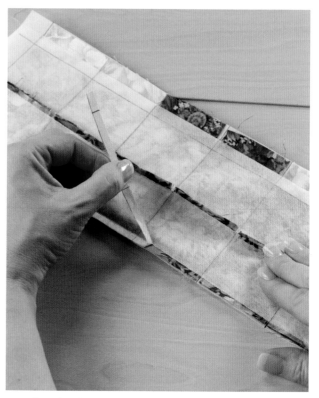

3 Flip the foundation to the back. Using small scissors or a seam ripper, slit the loop of the foundation open. Lay the piece flat, grasp some of the foundation, and tear it out of the seam allowance. It should tear off very easily.

Pressing Needs

1 Press seams right sides together to set them. Use a warm iron, no steam.

2 Press seams in opposite directions. Begin on one end and press the seams in the first row west. Fold this pressed row underneath the patchwork so that the second row is now at the end.

3 Press the seams in the second row east. Make sure that you start on the same side of both of your sections of foundation, pressing in the same direction so that when you sew them together, the seam allowances are in a uniform direction.

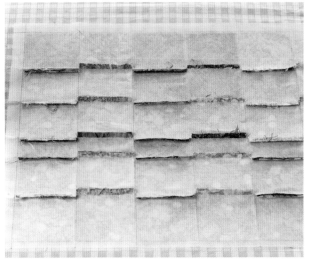

4 Continue pressing the seams as indicated until the rows are finished.

7 Fold and sew your last batch of seams.

8 Remove the foundation from the seam allowances. It is usually not necessary to slit each loop open before it can be torn away. Gently dig at one corner with your scissors, grasp the foundation and pull. (This stage can get tedious, but you are almost done!)

9 Press your seams right sides together to set them. Then press in whichever way you prefer. (Press seams toward an object you want to pop out a bit from the surface, such as a tree trunk or fence rail.)

10 Add any appliqué that the pattern calls for.

11 Add borders if desired.

12 When the quilt top is complete, remove the remaining foundation. It is not necessary to remove every fluff.

5 Sew the foundation sections together. Carefully trim on the last grid lines where the two sections will be adjoined. You will be sewing ¼" from this edge; trim carefully. Don't bother trimming any of the other ends at this time. Lay the two sections right sides together, aligning and pinning the drawn grid lines together. Sew with tiny stitches, then remove the foundation in this seam, and press the allowances in a uniform direction with the rest of the quilt top.

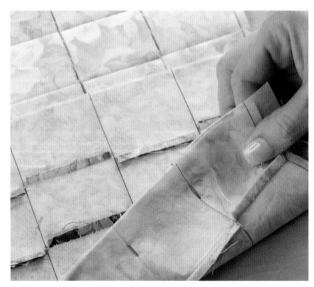

6 Match the grid lines, top and bottom.

Large Quilts

Some of the patterns in this book will require between six and 10 sections of foundation. The best way to construct these larger wall hangings is to fold and sew sections into long rows. After each row is complete, combine the rows.

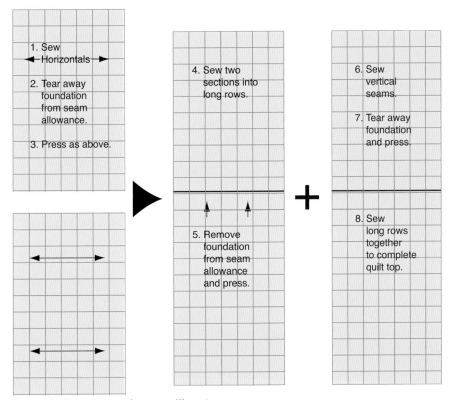

1. Sew Horizontals
2. Tear away foundation from seam allowance.
3. Press as above.

4. Sew two sections into long rows.

5. Remove foundation from seam allowance and press.

6. Sew vertical seams.
7. Tear away foundation and press.

8. Sew long rows together to complete quilt top.

Sew multiple sections in larger wallhangings.

Handler Textile Corporation (HTC) makes three foundations that work well. These are widely available at quilt shops (see Resources on page 127).

- **Rinse-Away** works well for small projects. Because it is lightweight, it cannot support large sections of glued fabric squares. It is also trickier to draw draft lines on, because it is not translucent, and you still must tear it away, as only the most vigorous washing will remove it.
- **Fundation** is a nice, lightweight stabilizer. It is quite translucent, so drafting is easy. It folds nicely, and if you are careful, it will support large sections of glued fabric squares.

It is a little more expensive than the other HTC foundations.

- **Tear-Away** is translucent and tears away cleanly and easily. It is strong enough to support larger projects as it is a little thicker and stiffer.

Hammer Brothers Foundations can be found at specialty sewing stores or online (see Resources on page 127).

- **Lightweight Tear-Away F-810** is a stronger, translucent foundation that works very well on larger, and therefore, heavier projects. It is available in other widths, so make sure you purchase the 21" size for projects in this book — you might have to call them directly for it (see Resources on page 127).

A "Bitter" Crossing, 51½" x 58½". Machine pieced, machine quilted and appliquéd. Exhibited at the Museum of American Quilter's Society "Lewis and Clark Expedition," Nashville, Tenn., and "Covering the Corps: Piece by Piece," National Historic Oregon Trail Interpretive Center, Baker City, Ore.

Chapter 4

Putting It All Together

In this chapter we will put it all together: adding appliqué, layering with tulle, painting with fabric dye markers and other special effects. We will also discuss adding borders, free-motion machine embroidery, fuse-basting and quilting. These are the tricks that can make your landscape quilt sing.

Adding Appliqué

So your quilt is put together now and waiting for your finishing touches. In many ways, this is the fun stuff! Appliqués can make your landscapes sparkle; they are simple to add to your stabilized quilt top and can add a touch of spontaneity. (Your foundation keeps your seams straight and helps prevent distortion during the fusing process.) For all fusible appliqué I recommend using Wonder Under fusible interfacing. Here are general steps for fusible appliqué:

1 If you want the appliquéd object to pop out a bit from the quilt top, layer a lightweight fusible interfacing to the wrong side of the fabric before you apply the fusible webbing. This technique creates a faux trapunto look in your larger flowers or butterflies. It also helps prevent the lumpy seams from showing through the appliqué.

2 Remove the fusible webbing's paper backing from the prepared fabric before you start cutting. (This keeps the edges in better condition.)

3 Score the fusible webbing's paper with scissors to peel it away from the fabric; don't try to separate it at the edge of the appliqué.

4 After arranging the appliqués on the quilt top, very lightly touch them with a hot iron to baste them in place. Then hang your quilt top on your design wall and view it from a distance.

5 When you are satisfied with your design, carefully carry your quilt top to your pressing surface and use steam to permanently bond the appliqués to the quilt top.

6 Stitch down the appliqués around their very edges. It will be more difficult to remove the last of the foundation if the appliqués have been stitched to it. While appliqués can be stitched down as part of the quilting process, sometimes this leads to an untidy quilt back. The best time for stitching is after the quilt top is fuse-basted to the batting and before the backing is added. (see fuse-basting, page 58).

Special Effects

Dye markers and watercolor pencils come in a wide variety of colors.

Markers and Pencils

These markers and pencils are wonderful tools. You can easily add shadows and create a natural, dimensional look. Start slow and practice before you touch a new dye marker to your quilt top. Remember, you can always appliqué something over a mistake if you make one! Many of the projects will use a touch or two of a dye marker; these are simple and easy to do. Just follow the picture patterns.

Watercolor pencils are great for subtle changes such as deepening the color of a print. Dye markers have a bolder dramatic color. To deepen a blue shade, for example, dip your paintbrush in water, touch it to the tip of your pencil and apply it to the fabric. Once dry, press it with a hot iron to set the color.

Using watercolor pencils is one way to deepen the shade of a fabric.

Often, light-colored leaf fabric will have a cream-colored background. To change the background to a sky blue, for example, lightly apply the marker and use a brush dipped in water to blend.

Slow-drying dye and a little water make it easy to change a light background color.

Layering Tulle

Layers of tulle add atmosphere to a landscape; they can also be used to hold items in place. Instead of appliqué, many types of leaves and flowers can be put under a layer of tulle, and then outline stitched in place. Tulle can also intensify or dull the colors beneath it. I will often try different colors of tulle before I settle on one for the layering. For example, a shade of violet tulle was used to give dimension to the window box in A Room with a View (page 113), and a warm apricot tulle was used to hold the flowers in place.

There are times when you will need a very special flower. If you can't find one on a fabric bolt, try your craft shop's floral department! The flowers you choose need to be flat. Carefully pull them off of the stems. Arrange the flowers in their positions, and layer the tulle on top. Pin the tulle in place and outline stitch. Cut away excess tulle.

When layering with tulle, it's important to keep the quilt top very flat. Make sure to press the quilt top thoroughly before pinning the tulle in place. The tulle can be layered and stitched before the foundation is removed from the back of the squares, or it can be layered and stitched once the quilt top is fused to the batting. For long or large pieces of tulle, it is better to stitch while the foundation is on, because the quilt top is still flat. Once the tulle is stitched in place, be very careful with a hot iron. Tulle melts if the iron even *looks* at it! Also, if you have any threads sticking out of your seams, remove them before the tulle goes on. (This I learned from the school of hard knocks.)

To layer tulle, keep things very flat and outline stitch. In this photo, the leaves were fused in place and the flowers are layered under tulle.

Adding Borders

Borders frame your landscapes and bring out their best colors; they lead the eye to the good stuff inside your picture. Leave the foundation on the back as you shop for border fabric. This will prevent the landscape from getting stretched or distorted as you carry it around. I strongly recommend starching your border fabric before cutting your strips. Adding that extra stability to a fabric can go a long way toward preventing curved seams. Setting your machine for smaller stitches can also be helpful in sewing long, straight seams.

Fuse-Basting

There are two major advantages to fusing your quilt top to your batting. The first is that your seams will be held in place during the quilting process. Often, free-motion quilting across multiple patches causes distortion in straight rows. The second advantage is that stitching down your appliqués halfway through the fuse-basting process creates a very tidy quilt back. Many art quilters are fusing their quilt tops and batting together for these very reasons. (The batt is not a solid piece; its fibers give and stretch during the quilting process; so your quilt will still be pliant.) Here are the steps to fuse-baste your quilt and stitch down your appliqués.

1 Remove the remaining foundation, and press the quilt top carefully.

2 Cut the batting roughly an 1" larger than the quilt top.

3 Gently tape the batting down on a large, flat surface, smoothing out any wrinkles.

4 Peel the fusible webbing from the paper backing and lay the webbing on the batting; fuse it to within 1" of the outside edge of your quilt top.

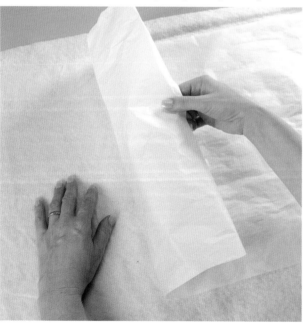

Separate the webbing from the paper at the edge. Hold down the webbing with your left hand and gently peel off the paper with your right hand.

5 Gently smooth your quilt on top of the fusible webbing, making sure all your seams are straight, your borders are at perfect 90-degree angles and the quilt top is flat.

6 Begin at the center and lightly press the quilt top, lifting the iron with an up-and-down motion, and working gently to outside edges. Do not slide the iron across the quilt, and do not use steam.

7 When the quilt has been lightly pressed and everything looks even, press it again using steam. Stitch down appliqués using a sharps 70/10 needle and monofilament thread. Add machine embroidery, if desired.

8 To fuse the backing, flip the quilt sandwich over and place small pieces of fusible webbing every 4" to 5" along the batting. (Think of the webbing pieces as your pins.)

9 Smooth on the quilt back, and lightly press it in the same way as in Steps 5 and 6.

10 Finish fusing using steam. When you are done creating your sandwich, you will notice that there appear to be gentle ripples here and there. If your quilt top and backing were smoothed on and flat, these slightly rippled areas are completely normal and will disappear in the quilting process. The batting will yield itself to the quilting process, and your quilt will hang nicely on the wall. If your batting got terribly bunched somehow, it is possible to tear it off of the quilt top and re-fuse it.

Adding Machine Embroidery

Because your quilt top is stabilized by your basted batting, many kinds of machine embroidery can be added to the surface with very little distortion. To add embroidery, place the top of your hoop beneath the portion of the quilt top to be embroidered. Gently push the bottom of the hoop into the top and tighten. Carefully pull your layers taut, but don't stretch them. It is not necessary to add more stabilizers to the top if the design is not densely stitched.

Detail, Autumn Triptych. Machine embroidery can add veins to leaves.

Quilting

Your quilting should reflect the natural environment you created with your fabric. Start by stitching in the ditch around your appliqués or around your land masses. When you get to areas that need filling, try to avoid the jigsaw puzzle-piece shapes that are so common with stipple quilting. Think shrubbery. It is more horizontal than it is vertical. Shrubbery also has many hues, which is why I strongly recommend quilting with variegated threads. Shrubbery quilting is also great for filler areas on hillsides or in a forest canopy.

Water and sky can be quilted with long, wavy horizontals. Try a variegated blue thread for your water ripples. Overlap your stitching lines, and bring in a light or white thread to highlight sunlit areas.

Quilt topographical lines in smooth areas.

Quilt topographical lines in smooth areas.

Detail, Autumn Triptych. Close-up of shrubbery quilting shapes.

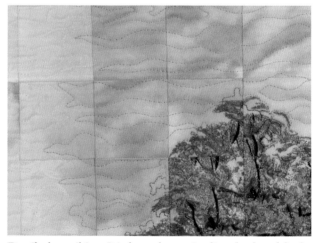

Detail, sky quilting. Stitch gently curving lines back and forth and around imaginary cloud shapes.

Quilting stitches can also be great for adding special touches, like curlicue vines and veins in leaves.

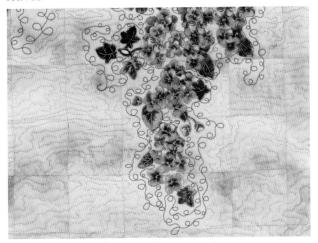

Detail, Terrace By the Sea curlicue vines. Sew loop-the-loops with dark green thread.

Back, Alaskan Nights. Mountain, sky and water quilting.

Blocking

Blocking is an important part of the finishing process. There are various glues and starches in your finished quilt, and during the blocking process, many of these substances are removed. When the quilting is finished, fill your washing machine with cold water, and gently push your quilt into the water. Let it soak for a few minutes and run your spin cycle to remove the water. Take your quilt to a flat surface and stretch it out in all directions until it lays flat. Measure and use your rotary ruler to make sure your borders are even and that your corners have right angles. If you are in a hurry for your quilt to dry, put a fan on it to expedite the drying process.

I usually block before I add my binding. After the quilt is dry, trim the borders if necessary and sew your binding on. I use a single-fold binding, as it makes a nicely mitered corner. When the binding

TIP

If you have a dark red fabric in your quilt top, either in the landscape itself or in the border fabric, do not soak your quilt. Instead lay it flat and mist it down with clean water. Mist the back first and then the quilt top.

is stitched down in back, wet the edges of the quilt again, and let them dry. This helps the quilt lay flat. The last few things you need to do to finish your quilt are to sign it, put a sleeve on it and hang it. Treat your quilt as you would a painting. Hanging it from a sleeve provides the best view and keeps your picture hanging smooth and straight.

Projects

The following projects are rated 1 through 3 by their level of ease or difficulty; this is to help you choose a project that will be successful. Projects with a rating of 1 are great for learning the fold-and-sew process. They are simple to construct and easy to choose fabrics for. Projects rated 2 are larger works that will require more fabric and more construction experience. Projects rated 3 require careful drafting and construction, more studied fabric choices and more blending capabilities. Please pay attention to the ratings and learn the process before you choose a complicated landscape.

Levels

1: Easy pattern requiring a few basic fabrics.

2: Larger quilt requiring multiple sections of foundation and greater fabric selection.

3: Project requires careful drafting and more foundation piecing. Patterns can also require more fabrics and blending capabilities.

A Word About Patterns

The patterns all require drafting a 2¼" grid with added sewing lines within the grid. The dashed green lines are your foundation layout patterns. The patterns also have the major design elements in a slightly bolder line to help you see where you are going as you draft and design. Follow the project photos for fabric layout. Have fun!

Garden Window

24½" x 24½"

No weeds will ever come up in this garden, there will be no dirt under your fingernails, and your flowers will always be at their peak! If you never have experienced the joy of cutting and pasting flowers in a free fall, you are in for a treat.

Fabrics

- 2 yd. 21"-22" foundation – 1 section will be 9 squares x 12 squares and the other will be 3 squares x 12 squares
- ½ yd. sky
- ⅛ yd. each, 3 different light to medium greens for meadow and hills
- 1 yd. steely gray for window frame, border, and binding
- ½ yd. assorted flowers, leaves, birds or butterflies. Some flowers can be tiny for appliqué in the meadow

Notions

- ½ yd. lightweight fusible interfacing, dark
- ½ yd. lightweight fusible interfacing, white
- 3 yd. fusible webbing
- Sewing needles, size 90/14 topstitch or universal and sharps 70/10
- Monofilament thread
- Acid-free glue sticks for paper projects

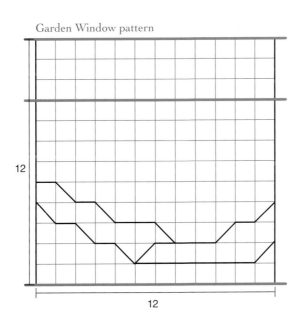

Garden Window pattern

12

12

Instructions

1 Draft the grid and diagonals onto your foundation sections.

2 Cut your sky and green fabrics into generous 2⅛" squares. Don't cut your flowers or leaf fabrics.

3 Arrange your fabrics according to the pattern, keeping your darkest green in the foreground and your lightest green in the background. Try to create a smooth, seamless sky along the horizon line.

4 When you are happy with your design, follow the instructions in Chapter 3 for sewing your quilt top together. Begin sewing with your half-square triangles. Before continuing with this pattern, remove the foundation from the last set of seams only; leave the rest of the foundation on the back of your fabric squares

5 Cut a 21" x 3" rectangle of the gray window frame fabric. Be sure to follow the grain lines of the print.

6 According to manufacturer's directions, fuse the dark interfacing to the backside of this rectangle. Attach fusible webbing to that.

7 Cut four ½" strips the length of the rectangle. Center these directly every four rows over the seams of your quilt top.

8 Lightly iron baste the strips in place. If necessary, use a T-square to make sure they are at perfect 90-degree angles to each other.

9 Fuse the strips in place.

10 Fuse white interfacing to the wrong side of your floral fabric. Next, attach the fusible webbing. If desired, fuse webbing to the wrong side of meadow flowers.

11 Now for the fun! Arrange flowers, leaves and butterflies — as many as you want — in a free fall on your windowpanes. Cut some flowers in half and place them next to the window frame for a neat effect.

12 Add your window frame borders (mine are 2½" finished). Remove the remaining foundation.

13 Fuse the quilt top to the batting. (See Chapter 4 for directions on fuse-basting.) Stitch down your appliqués using monofilament thread and sharps 70/10 needle. Use a dark green thread to add green stems for the flowers in the foreground meadow.

14 Fuse on backing and quilt; add curlicue vines if desired.

15 Bind, add a sleeve and hang your quilt in a place where you can enjoy it!

Creating a 3-dimensional effect.

Fence Post ^{LEVEL} 1

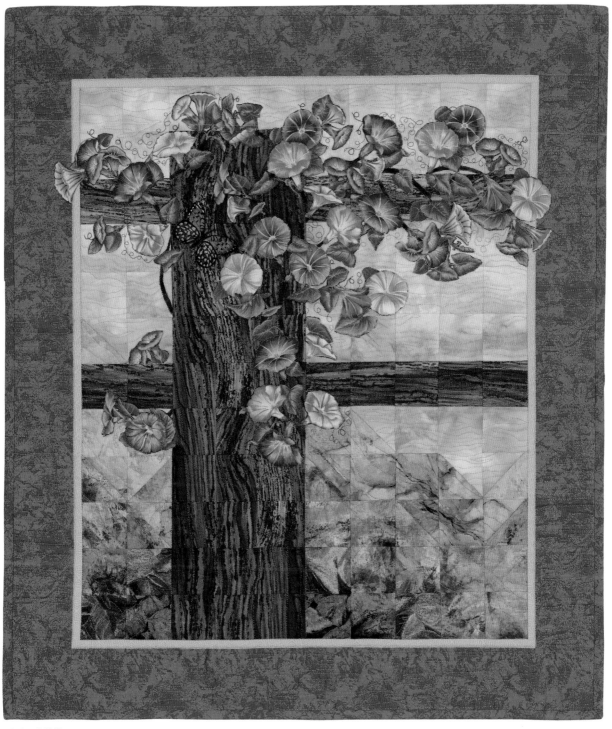

23" x 26½"

I love the look of old-fashioned morning glory vines as they clamber their way up to the sunshine. I also love mountains and blue skies, so I combined them into one of my favorite wall hangings. This is a great project for a beginner.

Fabrics

- 2 yd. 21"-22" foundation – 1 section will be 9 squares x 10 squares and the other section will be 3 squares x 10 squares
- ⅛ yd. gray for mountains
- ½ yd. sky
- ⅓ yd. wood grain
- ¼ yd. assorted green prints. These can be just one or two mottled, vaguely leafy green prints, light to medium in value. (Check out the back side of your prints – they might be perfect.)
- ½ yd. flowers and leaves for appliqué
- Scrap of dark green for vines and branches
- Butterfly or hummingbird for appliqué

Notions

- 3 yd. fusible webbing
- 1 yd. lightweight fusible interfacing, white
- Sewing needles, size 90/14 topstitch or universal and sharps 70/10
- Monofilament thread
- Acid-free glue sticks for paper projects

Fence Post pattern

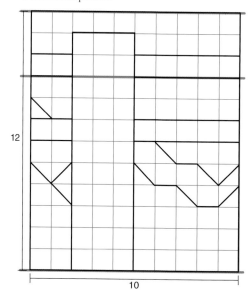

12

10

Instructions

1 Draft the grid onto your foundation sections according to the pattern.

2 Cut your fabrics into generous 2⅛" squares.

3 Arrange the fabric squares according to the pattern. Begin with the fence post. You may want to use the back side of your wood-grain fabric for the rails. Keep the darkest portions of your green prints in the foreground. Create a smooth sky near the horizon line.

4 When you are happy with your design, follow the instructions in Chapter 3 for sewing your quilt top together. Begin sewing with your half-square triangles. Before continuing with this pattern, remove the foundation from the last set of seams only; leave the rest of the foundation on the back of your fabric squares.

5 Following the manufacturer's directions, fuse the interfacing to the wrong side of your floral fabric, and attach the fusible webbing. Fuse more webbing to the wrong side of your dark green scraps, and cut out long, curved, skinny pieces for the vine and branches. (My vines curl around from the backside of the fence post.)

6 Cut out your flowers, leaves and vines. Arrange them on and around the fence post.

7 Attach fusible interfacing and webbing to the back side of your butterfly or hummingbird. Go ahead and place it in with the flowers.

8 When you are satisfied with your design, fuse everything in place, and sew on your borders.

9 Add a few more flowers to reach into the border area. Fuse these in place.

10 Remove the remaining foundation from the back of the squares.

11 Fuse the quilt top to the batting according to the instructions in Chapter 4.

12 Using monofilament thread, stitch down your appliqués using a sharps 70/10 needle.

13 Fuse on the backing, and quilt as desired, adding curlicue vines for a natural look.

14 Bind, label and hang your treasure!

Detail of flowers and butterfly.

Daffodil Meadow

LEVEL
1

25" x 20"

Sometimes on rainy spring days, bright yellow daffodils are the only sunshine we get! You don't need to use daffodils. Any medium-size meadow flower will work well in this design. This is the first pattern where the inner border will be pieced along with the rest of the quilt top.

Fabrics
- 2 yd. 21"-22" foundation — 1 section will be 9 squares x 12 squares and the other section will be 6 squares x 12 squares
- ½ yd. sky
- ⅓ yd. dark meadow print
- ⅛ yd. medium meadow print
- ⅛ yd. light green meadow print
- ⅛ yd. coordinating inner border color
- Scraps, assorted green for stems
- Tiny meadow flowers to appliqué at the base of daffodil clumps
- ⅓ yd. daffodil print or any other floral you might like to play with

Notions
- ½ yd. lightweight fusible interfacing; white for light flowers, dark if you choose dark flowers
- 3 yd. fusible webbing
- Sewing needles, size 90/14 topstitch or universal and sharps 70/10
- Acid-free glue sticks for paper projects
- Monofilament thread

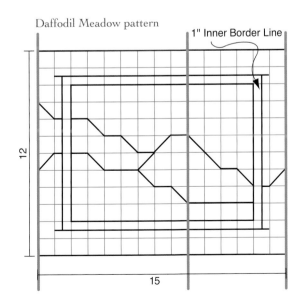

Daffodil Meadow pattern

1" Inner Border Line

12

15

Instructions

1 Draft grid lines, diagonals and inner border rectangles onto foundation sections according to the pattern. The inner border line is 1" from the second grid line on the outside edges of your grid.

2 Cut the inner border fabric into 2⅛" strips. Cut these strips into 1½" rectangles.

3 Cut your meadow prints into generous 2⅛" squares.

4 Arrange your squares according to the pattern, keeping the darkest portions of your medium meadow print nearest the lightest portions of your dark meadow print. Pin your diagonals and rectangles into place as needed.

5 When you are happy with your design, follow the instructions in Chapter 3 for sewing your quilt top together. Begin sewing with your half-square triangles and rectangles. Before continuing with this pattern, remove the foundation from the last set of seams only; leave the rest of the foundation on the back of your fabric squares.

6 Fuse interfacing to the wrong side of the daffodil fabric, and then apply fusible webbing to that. Fuse webbing to the wrong side of the green scraps and tiny meadow print.

7 Cut out the daffodil flower heads, skinny stems for the daffodils and clumps of tiny flowers.

8 Arrange daffodils and stems. Fuse in place. Add clumps of meadow flowers and fuse in place.

9 Remove the rest of the foundation. Press flat.

10 Fuse the quilt top to the batting, and stitch down your appliqués using a sharps 70/10 needle and monofilament thread.(See Chapter 4 for directions on fuse-basting).

11 Fuse the backing to the batting and quilt as desired.

12 Bind, label, hang and enjoy your quilt.

Blending fabrics from light to dark.

Covenant Cross

38"x 32"

This landscape is rich with symbolic meaning. In this very painterly quilt, you will have the opportunity to create a more traditional watercolor quilt, blending values and using primarily floral fabrics. The rainbow of the covenant is appliquéd after the quilt top is constructed, as are the red flowers and leaves at the base of the cross. Pay careful attention to the pattern; the inner border is added between your regular grid squares.

Fabrics

- 4 yd. 21"-22" foundation – 4 sections will be 9 squares x 10 squares, and 2 sections will be 6 squares x 10 squares
- 1 yd. total of 2 to 3 different light florals for sky
- ⅛ yd. distant hill behind the cross
- ¼ yd. light green meadow print
- ¼ yd. each of 3 different brown prints for cross and inner border
- ¾ yd. total of 1 to 2 different dark green meadow prints
- ¼ yd. floral fabrics for rainbow
- Scraps for the following at the base of the cross:
  Red for small flowers
  Green for small leaves

Notions

- 6½ yd. fusible webbing
- Sewing needles size 90/14 topstitch or universal and sharps 70/10
- Monofilament thread
- Acid-free glue sticks for paper projects

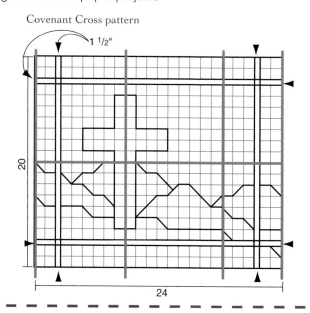

Covenant Cross pattern

1 1/2"

20

24

74

A word about fabrics

Find floral fabrics that blend lighter into darker tones. I strongly recommend buying fabrics that have a back side that may also be useable. The green hills are the same fabric; the back side is used for one hill. The blue border and hills use three fabrics; I use the front and back of each to add texture and value. Look for medium-sized prints and soft, light florals for your sky. Look for medium to large multicolored brown prints for the cross; the prints should have plenty of design variation and range from medium to dark in value.

Instructions

1 Draft your grid pattern according to the pattern. Your inner border is added between your regular grid squares in this pattern.

2 Cut your fabrics into generous 2⅛" squares. Cut your brown prints into strips, and from these strips, only cut enough squares to complete the cross.

3 Arrange your fabrics, beginning with the cross and foreground. Keep the darkest of your brown prints toward the bottom left portion of the cross and the lightest to the upper right. If you were able to find a light floral fabric that has some yellow, place it in a sun-shaped pattern, and blend it into your other sky fabrics. Keep the darkest of your blue prints for the base of the hill and the upper border area. Blend these darker values into lighter blues for the top of the blue mountain and the border sides.

4 Cut your remaining brown strips into 1½" rectangles and arrange these to mirror the diagonal light pattern in the cross. (See Covenant Cross photo). Cut more strips and rectangles as needed to complete your landscape.

5 When you are happy with your design, follow the instructions in Chapter 3 for sewing your quilt top together. Begin sewing with your half-square triangles. Before continuing with this pattern, remove the foundation from the last set of seams only; leave the rest of the foundation on the back of your fabric squares.

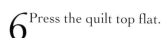

6 Press the quilt top flat.

7 Attach fusible webbing to the wrong side of your small red flowers, leaves and floral rainbow fabrics. Peel off the paper backing.

8 Cut out your red flowers and leaves, and create plants at the foot of the cross. Blend these into meadow area as desired. Fuse in place.

9 Cut out your flowers, and design a rainbow. Fuse in place.

10 Remove the remaining foundation and press again.

11 Fuse the quilt top to batting, and stitch down the appliqués using sharps 70/10 and monofilament thread.

12 Fuse on the backing. Quilt, adding curlicues to the rainbow and rays in the sun if desired.

13 Add a sleeve, sign your quilt and hang it where it will be enjoyed!

Detail of cross and rainbow.

A Lake Superior Maple

LEVEL **2**

27" x 31"

You get to play with warm and cold color contrasts in this little quilt. Tulle is used to create the illusion of dark, cold water in the foreground. For this maple tree, you will need to choose a leaf fabric that is lighter in value so it fits with the sky. Maple leaves printed on black or very dark backgrounds will not work well with this design.

Fabrics

- 2 yd. 21"-22" foundation — 1 section will be 9 squares x 12 squares and the other will be 6 squares x 12 squares
- ¼ yd. water
- ¼ yd. sky
- ⅛ yd. trunk
- ¼ yd. green for ground
- ½ yd. maple leaves
- ¼ yd. royal blue tulle
- ¼ yd. white tulle
- Scraps, yellow and red, for leaves

Notions

- Monofilament thread
- Sewing needles, size 90/14 topstitch or universal and sharps 70/10
- Acid-free glue sticks for paper projects
- 3 yd. fusible webbing

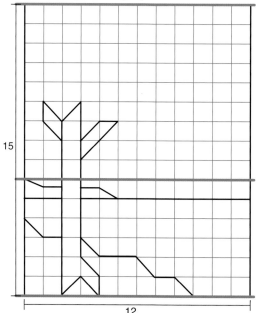

A Lake Superior Maple pattern

15

12

Instructions

1 Draft the grid on your foundation according to the pattern. Pay careful attention to the scalene triangles; their widths are 1⅛", or half the width of the squares. (Reread drafting scalene triangles in Chapter 3 if necessary.)

2 Cut your fabrics into generous 2⅛" squares. Do not cut up all of your leaf fabric.

3 Arrange your fabrics according to the pattern, pinning triangles into place as necessary.

4 If desired, create peek-a-boo in your maple leaves. Create this effect by cutting out tiny portions in the centers of the leaf fabric squares. Lightly glue pieces of the sky fabric on the back. When the glue is dry, stitch the cut-out edges of the leaf fabric using monofilament thread and sharps 70/10 needle. Place the finished fabric squares in with the canopy.

5 When you are happy with your design, follow the instructions in Chapter 3 for sewing your quilt top together. Begin sewing with your half-square triangles, scalene triangles and rectangles. Before continuing with this pattern, remove the foundation from the last set of seams only. Leave the rest of the foundation on the back of your fabric squares.

6 Press your quilt top flat.

7 Lay your white tulle over the horizon line where the water meets the sky. If your tulle is rumpled, press it with steam using a press cloth; tulle melts easily!

8 Pin the tulle in place, keeping everything flat. See Chapter 4, Layering Tulle, for additional instructions.

9 Stitch in the ditch along the sky side of the water. Use tiny stitches with monofilament thread on top, white thread in the bobbin, and a sharps 70/10 size needle.

10 Stitch a long, wavy horizontal line, varying from ½" to 1" along the water side of the horizon line. Be sure to enclose the tulle on all sides by stitching in the ditch along the affected portions of the tree trunk. Don't bother placing any tulle on the left side of the tree. Trim away excess tulle.

11 Layer royal blue tulle over the portion of the water closest to the land and halfway up the width of the lake. Pin in place.

12 Stitch in the ditch along the land where it meets the water.

Peek-a-boo blue cut-outs and appliqué are an easy way to blend the canopy and sky.

13 Stitch a long, wavy horizontal line across the top of the tulle, completely enclosing it at both the side of the quilt top and the tree trunk. Trim away excess tulle.

14 To make the water extra cold, deep and blue, add another layer of royal blue tulle half the width of the first layer. Trim.

15 Apply some of the fusible webbing to a portion of your maple leaf fabric. You won't need more than ⅛ yd. Fuse more webbing to the back of your red and yellow leaf scraps.

16 Cut out leafy shapes and random leaves from your maple fabric. Place these over the trunk and branches and to soften the edge of your tree canopy and sky. Fuse in place, being careful not to touch the iron to the tulle.

17 Cut out and arrange leaves on the ground and up the tree trunk. Fuse in place using a press cloth.

18 Add borders and remove the foundation. Don't worry about getting all the tufts of foundation off. (Border tips and advice can be found in Chapter 4.)

19 Fuse the quilt top to the batting using a press cloth and stitch down your appliqués using monofilament thread and sharps 70/10 needle. Use contrasting thread to create veins in the vine leaves.

20 Fuse batting to backing. Quilt as desired using a variegated blue thread to quilt long, wavy horizontals in the water.

21 Bind, hang and enjoy!

Barn Doors LEVEL **2**

37½" x 30½"

Red barns and concrete silos dot the countryside around my home. Here is an easy pattern where you can mix the traditional barn door block with the real thing! Flowers are appliquéd two different ways, both by fusing and with a tulle overlay. You will also get your first taste of using fabric dye markers to shade the wood trim and watercolor pencils to deepen the tones of your blocks.

Fabrics

- 2 yd. 21"-22" foundation — 2 sections each of 9 squares x 14 squares
- ⅛ yd. shingle
- ¼ yd. red barn
- ¼ yd. dark leafy green
- ¼ yd. medium grassy green
- ¼ yd. light green
- ⅛ yd. green print — optional — to add texture to the meadow in front of the barn
- ⅛ yd. concrete-looking print for silo
- ⅛ yd. fence post
- ½ yd. total of 6 to 7 sky blues ranging from light to medium. Scraps are fine; the more the merrier!
- Scraps

  Gray for silo roof and windows

  Cream for wood trim

  Green for leaves

  Brown for tree branches

  A crab apple blossom fabric or one with small white flowers, for approximately 15 to 20 flowers

  Farm animals – cows and chickens (or pigs, ducks, etc!)

  Tiny flowers for fence post (optional)

Notions

- 1 yd. fusible interfacing, white
- 4 yd. fusible webbing
- Gray fabric dye marker
- Watercolor pencil, dark blue if necessary for darker blue patches
- Monofilament and lingerie threads
- Sewing needles, size 90/14 topstitch or universal, and sharps 70/10
- Acid-free glue sticks for paper projects

  *Fence post flowers can be from a scrap, or they can be silk (See Chapter 4 for details about how to use silk flowers).

Barn Doors pattern

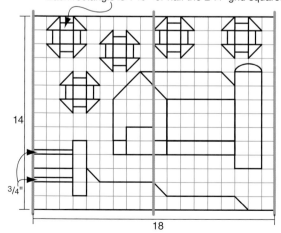

Each rectangle is 1⅛" or half the 2¼" grid square.

14

3/4"

18

Instructions

1 Draft your foundation according to the pattern, adding ¾" rails for fence and barn door block diagonals. The rectangles for the blocks are 1⅛" (half the size of the square).

2 Cut your fabrics into generous 2⅛" squares.

3 Arrange your fabric squares using the color pattern for a guide. As you place your sky blues; keep the lightest of your fabrics closest to the horizon, and use your mediums for the barn door blocks in this portion of the sky. Arrange your medium sky fabrics in the upper corners of the sky, using your darkest sky prints for the barn door blocks in these portions.

4 Check the contrast between your barn door blocks and the sky. If you find that your blocks disappear, you have two choices. The first is to rearrange, placing lighter sky fabrics around the blocks. If you like your deeper blue sky, there is another option: paint your blocks a deeper shade of blue using a watercolor pencil (I chose this option). See Chapter 4 for details. The process is extremely easy and the watercolor pencils are inexpensive and readily available at craft stores.

5 When you are happy with your design, follow the instructions in Chapter 3 for sewing your quilt top together. Begin sewing with your half-square triangles and rectangles. Before continuing with this pattern, remove the foundation from the last set of seams only; leave the rest of the foundation on the back of your fabric squares.

6 Fuse interfacing to the wrong side of cream fabric. Apply fusible webbing to this.

7 Cut barn trim from your prepared fabric, cutting ¼" strips for the nearest corner, the horizontal roof line, barn door trim and the X design. Cut ⅛" strips for the angled roof lines, and the farthest corner. Cut scant ⅛" strips for the upper window trim and set this aside. Arrange the rest and fuse in place.

8 Attach fusible webbing to the wrong side of your gray window fabric, green leaf scrap, tree branch scrap, spring blossom fabric, silo fabric and farm animals.

9 Cut out five ¾" x 1" pieces for barn windows and one 1" x 1¾" upper window. Arrange and fuse in place, adding set-aside trim to complete the upper window.

10 Cut out and arrange a few leaves to the fence post and rails. Arrange animals and fuse it in place.

11 Cut out the bent tree branch shape, which is approximately ¼" x 6". Arrange branches and blossoms; fuse them in place.

12 Dot a few of the tiny flowers on the fence post; if they are fabric, fuse them to the quilt top. If they are silk, follow directions in Chapter 4.

13 Stitch down your appliquéd barn trim, using sharps 70/10 needle and monofilament thread.

14 Sew your borders to your quilt top. Press carefully; avoid touching the iron to your tulle!

15 Using a gray dye marker, lightly shade the edges of your trim.

Detail of the barn door. Shading with a gray dye marker adds dimension to the wood trim.

16 Remove the rest of the foundation, and fuse your quilt top to the batting. Be very careful to use a press cloth over any areas of tulle.

17 Stitch down the rest of your appliquéd flowers and branches using your sharps 70/10 needle and monofilament thread.

18 Fuse on your backing, quilt and if desired, add beads to the center of your silk flowers.

19 Bind, label, hang and enjoy.

Silo Pattern

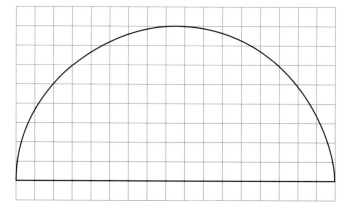

St. Mary Aspen

LEVEL
2

32" x 37"

Glacier National Park has been described as the jewel of North America, and St. Mary Lake is the most photographed lake in the Park. While the mountains surrounding this lake are simply breathtaking, the poor aspen trees take the brunt of harsh winds bellowing down off their peaks. Thread painting and fabric dye markers help to capture the distress of these poor trees. You will need a 35" cutting mat to accommodate the length of foundation required for this pattern.

Fabrics

- 2 yd. 21"-22" foundation — 2 sections each of 9 squares x 15 squares
- ⅓ yd. sky fabric
- ⅛ yd. each of 8 different gray prints (2 lights, 4 mediums, 2 darks)
- ¼ yd. each of 2 different green prints
- ¼ yd. each of 2 aspen trunk fabrics, one lighter than the other
- ⅛ yd. lake print
- ¼ yd. ground print
- ¼ yd. gold and orange print (or can be a variety of prints)
- Scrap of bright yellow print
- Red or orange tulle (optional)

Notions

- 3 yd. fusible webbing
- Sewing needles, size 90/14 topstitch or universal and sharps 70/10
- Acid-free glue stick for paper
- Assorted bright yellow and red threads for leafy canopy
- Variegated grassy green thread for thread painting on the ground
- Freezer paper
- Fabric dye marker, gray
- Ultra fine point permanent marker, black
- Machine embroidery hoop

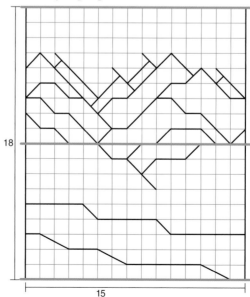

St. Mary Aspen pattern

18

15

Instructions

1 Draft your grid according to the pattern. Give careful attention to the scalene triangles along the lake shore. Draft these triangles one-half the width of the square. (Reread Chapter 3 if necessary). When you set up your foundation, place it over your 0" measuring line in order to get 15 squares length.

2 Cut your fabrics into generous 2⅛" squares.

3 Arrange your fabrics according to the pattern. Refer to the project photograph for your guide as you design your mountains.

4 When you are happy with your design, follow the instructions in Chapter 3 for sewing your quilt top together. Begin sewing with your half-square and scalene triangles. Before continuing with this pattern, remove the foundation from the last set of seams only. Leave the rest of the foundation on the back of your fabric squares.

5 Apply fusible webbing to the wrong side of your gold and yellow scrap fabrics and both portions of the aspen trunk fabric. Don't peel off the paper!

6 Trace aspen trunk patterns onto freezer paper. Cut out individual trees.

7 Peel the paper off of your gold and yellow scraps. Cut out curvy, irregular (think elongated jigsaw puzzle) pieces. Scatter a few of these shapes into the canopy portion of your landscape.

8 Arrange your freezer paper trees onto your prepared aspen trunk fabrics. Using a hot iron, press the paper patterns to the right side of the fabrics.

9 Using a pencil, lightly trace the trunk shapes onto the aspen fabric, and carefully peel off the freezer paper trees. Cut out the fabric trees; continue to press and cut out as many freezer paper trees as desired of both the trunk prints. These tree shapes are reversible; just press them to the side with the fusible webbing, trace and cut out in the same manner. In this way, you can build up a wide variety of trunk shapes and heights.

10 Arrange some of your trunks over the tree canopy shapes. Fuse in place.

11 Continue to add trunks and shapes, building a small forest in a collage-like manner. Fuse in place.

12 Using dye markers, shade all of your tree trunks on the same side. (Mine are all shaded on the left side.)

13 Add the borders.

14 Remove the remaining foundation and fuse the quilt top to the batting. Stitch down your tree trunks using a sharps 70/10 needle and monofilament thread.

15 Position the top of your embroidery hoop under a portion of your foreground. Push the bottom ring down into the top ring, and tighten the hoop screws. Keep your quilt top fairly taut, but don't stretch it out by pulling it tight.

16 Using variegated green thread, free-motion stitch grassy portions, going over the patches as many times as you wish for a fuller effect. Stitching is not difficult! Begin by taking a few stitches in a north direction. Stop and come back south. As you do this, slowly move your quilt top to the east or west. If you wish, create a practice quilt sandwich and try your hand at it first. For added depth, highlight some areas with a dark green thread.

17 Stitch down your appliqué shapes in the tree canopy. If desired, layer canopy with small bits of red or orange tulle. (See Chapter 4, Layering Tulle).

18 To add texture, scribble stitch over your appliqués with contrasting thread. Stitch stipple shapes with gold and yellow threads.

19 Fuse on your backing. Quilt as desired. Add a sleeve, hang and enjoy!

Detail of the grasses and scribble-stitched trees

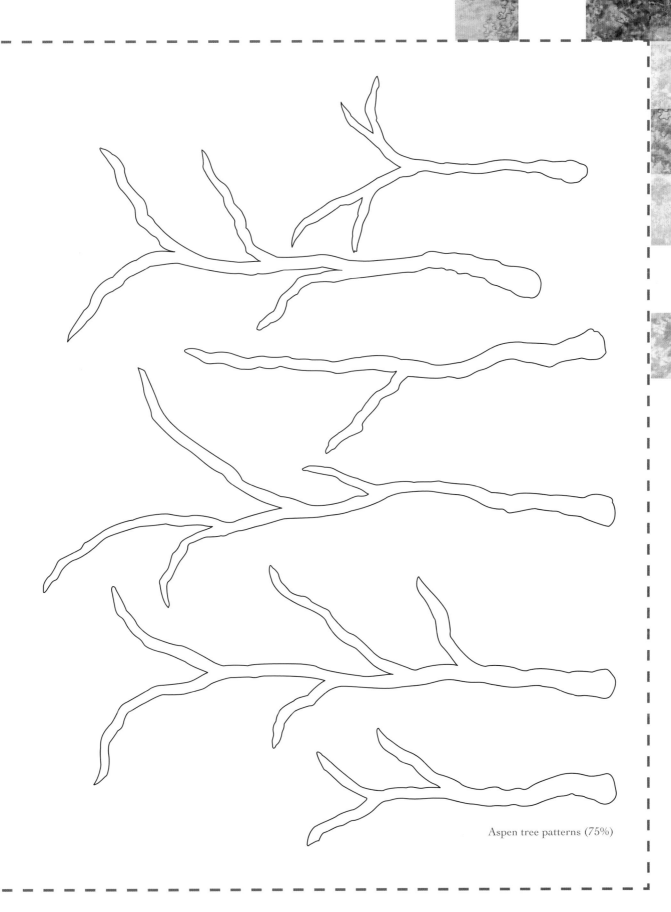

Aspen tree patterns (75%)

Spring's Call LEVEL 2

52" x 45"

Who can resist wandering down the path when the violets are blooming and the sun is shining? This quilt was accepted into the American Quilter's Society 2004 show in Paducah, Ky. It is machine pieced and machine quilted. The violet is Wisconsin's state flower, and I sprinkled them liberally all over the foreground.

Fabrics

- 4 yd. 21"-22" foundation — 4 sections will be 9 x 10 squares and 2 will be 6 x 10 squares
- ½ yd. dark brown tree trunk print
- ½ yd. medium brown tree trunk print
- ½ yd. of 2 dark to medium green forest floor prints
- ¼ yd. medium green meadow print
- ¼ yd. light meadow print
- ⅛ yd. path print
- ¼ yd. sky
- 1 yd. large tree leaf print – medium to dark values
- ½ yd. medium tree leaf print – medium to light values
- ½ yd. tiny leaf print – medium to light values
- ¼ yd. violets or some small flower print to appliqué on the forest floor
- ⅛ yd. blue-green calico to mix in canopy (optional)

Notions

- Acid-free glue sticks for paper projects
- 6 yd. fusible webbing
- Monofilament thread
- Sewing needles, size 90/14 topstitch or universal and sharps 70/10
- Fabric dye markers, black, brown and gray

A Word About Fabrics

As you shop for your fabrics, be on the lookout for scenic landscape prints that can provide a ready-made backdrop for your trees. If you can't find one single print that combines both a path and the forest floor, don't panic. You can cut and fuse portions of the meadow fabric over the edges of the path once the quilt top is pieced. The same technique can be used to blend the canopy and sky. A simple cut-up leafy fabric will work great as the forest floor, because we are adding appliquéd violets for variety and texture.

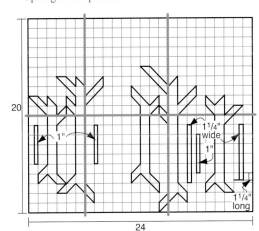

Spring's Call pattern

Instructions

1 Draft foundation sections according to the pattern; label each section to help you keep track of them. Label the top left section 1a and bottom left section 1b, etc. Add the sewing lines for your half-square triangles and rectangles.

2 Cut your fabrics into generous 2⅛" squares. Only cut one strip of your large leaf fabric at this point.

3 Arrange your fabrics, keeping the darkest of the green prints in the foreground. Place your path prints according to the picture. If you don't have any fabric prints containing both sandy brown and green to make this path, just arrange your sandy brown prints for now, placing the lightest sandy tones toward the horizon.

As you arrange your tree trunks, keep the lightest of the brown prints for the distant trunks. Blend the lightest of your meadow prints and your canopy prints together at the horizon line. If you would like an opening in the sky, once again you can appliqué portions of the light canopy and meadow prints to the sky prints to blend and soften any lines.

As you design your canopy, look at the way your large leaf print is cut. You might need to fussy-cut particular leaf patterns instead of strip-cutting the entire yard. Notice how my large leaves are fussy-cut and placed together to create one large leaf? This adds an illusion of depth and gives added interest to the canopy. Leaves can be fussy-cut by using a rotary ruler or by creating a transparent plastic template and drawing cutting lines on your fabric.

4 When you are happy with your design, follow the instructions in Chapter 3 for sewing your quilt top together. Please reread the Large Quilts section in Chapter 3 (page 51) for details. Before continuing with this pattern, remove the foundation from the last set of seams only; leave the rest of the foundation on the back of your fabric squares.

5 Apply fusible webbing to the wrong side of violets or other small flowers. Cut out clumps and fuse them to the forest floor.

6 If necessary, attach fusible webbing to the wrong side of the forest floor print. Cut out portions and fuse over the edges of your path to create a smooth transition. Do the same to blend the canopy and sky if needed.

7 Add your border fabric and fuse some more flowers into the border area. (Those violets will take over everything if you let them!)

8 Choose one side of each tree. Using fabric dye markers, lightly shade the trunks. Start with the gray, and once the fabric is wet, add a slight touch of black or brown. Practice on a scrap of fabric if you are unsure.

9 Remove the rest of the foundation and press the quilt top flat. Fuse the quilt top to batting and stitch down your appliqués using monofilament thread and sharps 70/10 needle.

10 Fuse backing to batting. Quilt as desired. Add intricate stipple quilting to distant shrubbery.

11 Add a sleeve, hang your quilt, and go for a walk in the fresh air!

Autumn Triptych

53½" x 40½"

Fall is my favorite season, and one of my favorite walks in the woods takes me by the remains of an early homesteader's foundation. Little did the poor farmers know that they were trying to cultivate an old glacial moraine – every season they grew a new crop of stones! This wall hanging was exhibited at the American Quilter's Society's 2005 show in Paducah, Ky.

Fabrics

- 6¼ yd. 21"-22" foundation – 6 sections will be 9 x 12 squares and 2 sections will be 5 x 12 squares
- 1½ yd. red border print
- 1½ yd. red and gold maple leaf print
- ½ yd. total 2 dark brown tree trunk prints
- ¼ yd. medium brown tree trunk print
- ½ yd. forest background
- ½ yd. of 2 forest floor prints
- ¼ yd. ferns or another leaf to appliqué
- ¼ yd. stone wall print (optional)
- ⅛ yd. bright golden leaves for sapling
- ⅛ yd. black for inner border
- Scrap of brown for sapling

Notions

- Sewing needles, size 90/14 topstitch or universal and sharps 70/10
- Monofilament thread
- Acid-free glue sticks for paper projects
- 6 yd. fusible webbing
- Fabric dye markers, black, gray, green and gold

A Word About Fabrics

If you would like to mix in more prints with the canopy, go right ahead! (See Maples and Aspen, page 18, for a mixed print look.) The forest floor in this quilt is a mix of very simple red and brown prints. Much of it will be a backdrop for the ferns, or another leaf if you prefer. The stone wall is optional; if you can't find the fabric, skip it! (The quilt's focal point is the sapling, not the stone wall behind it.) If you do find a fabric that works, appliqué bits of leaves, etc., to blend it into the forest floor.

Autumn Triptych pattern

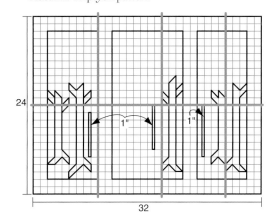

Instructions

1 Draft your grid and label your sections — top left as 1a, bottom left as 1b, etc.

2 Cut your fabrics into generous 2⅛" squares. Do not cut up all of your maple leaf fabric! Just cut ½ yd. or so and cut more strips and squares as needed.

3 Arrange your fabrics according to the pattern. Don't worry about blending your large leafy canopy print in with the forest background print. We will appliqué bits of the canopy over the background and fuse them in place once the quilt top is constructed. Keep your darkest trunk fabrics in the foreground and your medium-value prints behind them.

4 When you're happy with your design, follow the instructions in Chapter 3 for sewing your quilt top together. Before continuing with this pattern, remove the foundation from the last set of seams only; leave the rest of the foundation on the back of your fabric squares.

5 Apply fusible webbing to the wrong side of your fern fabric, your remaining maple leaf fabric and your black fabric.

Highlight ferns with green and gold fabric markers. Shade one side of your tree trunks with black and gray.

6 Cut long ¼" made strips of your black fabric and fuse them to create an inner border.

7 Cut out the ferns, and arrange them on the forest floor. They should fan into the space around them, including the border area. Fuse them in place.

8 Cut out portions of the maple leaves. Arrange them to soften the line between the tree canopy and the forest background. Fuse in place.

9 Choose the same side of each tree and, using fabric dye markers, lightly shade all of the trunks. Start shading with the dark gray marker, and when the fabric is damp, lightly bring in the black. Practice on a scrap if you are unsure.

10 Use the green and gold markers to enrich the color of the ferns and to add dimension to the veins.

11 Remove the remaining foundation, and press the quilt top flat.

12 Fuse the quilt top to batting, and stitch down your appliqués using the sharps 70/10 needle and monofilament thread. Add veins in the leaves and grasses to your forest floor as desired.

13 Fuse the backing to batting and quilt as desired. Add the binding and sleeve, hang and enjoy!

Sapling pattern (75%)

River Park with Birches

40½" x 32½"

Here is a quilt made with a lovely scenic landscape print, which is Michael Miller Fabric's "Park" print. We make it personal by appliquéing birch trees and leaves to the foreground. The repeat is every 24", and if you find another large scenic print, you can build a different landscape using the same techniques you'll learn in this one.

Fabrics

- 3 yd. 21"-22" foundation – 2 sections will be 9 squares x 15 squares and 1 section will be 2 squares x 15 squares
- 2 yd. Michael Miller Park print or similar large print with at least 4 repeats
- ½ yd. creamy gray birch trunk print
- ¼ yd. gold leaves for appliqué

Notions

- Monofilament thread
- 1 yd. fusible interfacing, light color if using light leaves
- 4 yd. fusible webbing
- Acid-free glue sticks for paper
- Sewing needles, size 90/14 topstitch or universal and sharps 70/10
- Fabric dye marker, gray
- Permanent ultra-fine point marker, black
- ½" strips of batting, one for each tree

A Word About Fabrics

There are lovely birch trunk fabrics available now. Look for Mary Mulari's Lake Superior Collection, or Natalie Sewell's Walk in the Woods, both by Marcus Brothers.

We will be freehand cutting, shading and stuffing our tree trunks; get ready to have fun!

River Park with Birches foundation chart — for pattern, see photo at left

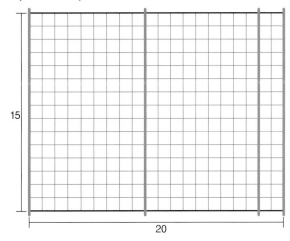

15

20

Instructions

1 Draft your grid according to the pattern layout. Lay out your foundation over the 0" inch measuring line on your large cutting mat to accommodate a grid of 15 squares.

2 Cut one of your pattern repeats into strips. Keep your strips in order and begin to cut your fabric strips into generous 2⅛" squares. It is important to center various landscape elements within your strips. Keep the edges of flowers or trees, for example, out of the seam allowances.

Cut strips as you go, keeping them in order.

3 Follow the photograph; build your landscape by arranging and cutting into your strips to stretch the picture across the surface of your landscape. Keep your prints in the order you cut them. I began with the tall reeds on the bottom left corner and worked my way across the bottom. The foreground area is filled in with extra portions from the dark trees and purple flowers. You will have to fussy-cut various motifs as necessary.

When you are finished with the foreground area, begin to work the middle and background. Enlarge the grassy area by cutting some squares from other repeats, and stretch out the water and shoreline in the same way. I also recreated the background trees by making the canopy open up more than the original design.

You may find that your left and right side forest backgrounds match each other; it is the repeat thing! Don't worry about this; we hide most of one side with our tree trunks and leaves. I also embellished the finished landscape by cutting out various bushes and flowers and fusing them to my quilt top to minimize this repetition.

4 When you are happy with your design, follow the instructions in Chapter 3 for sewing your quilt top together. Before continuing with this pattern, remove the foundation from the last set of seams only; leave the rest of the foundation on the back of your fabric squares.

5 Cut your trunk fabric to a length of 27". This is the height of the trees. Keep your bark pattern horizontal to this height. Check out the back side of your print; is it a lighter version than the front side? If so, cut it into two 27" lengths. If not, skip to Step 6.

6 Fuse interfacing to the wrong side of your trunk fabric. If you have two 27" lengths, make sure you fuse the interfacing to the right side of one of these lengths!

7 Using a large rotary mat and a sharp cutter, cut out some trunks. Start with the base of the tree and make your first cut ¼" from the left side of your fabric. Carefully cut your way up the tree, gradually moving your blade slightly to the right so that the top of your tree is narrower than the bottom. Start the second cut at the base of your tree, approximately 1½" to 2" away from your first cut. Slowly move up the tree, keeping your blade parallel to the first cut and gradually tapering the trunk to an inch or so at the top of the tree.

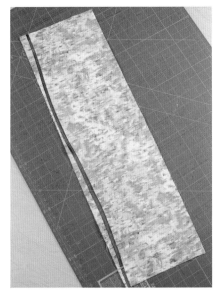

Try not to cut a straight line with your first cut.

What happens to one side of the tree happens to the other side. Keep your cuts parallel.

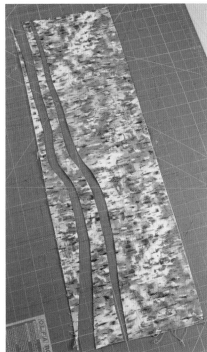

Not all birch trees are straight and true. Give them some elbows here and there.

8 Arrange your trunks on the quilt. Pin them in place.

9 Using monofilament thread and your sharps 70/10 needle, stitch one side of each of your trunks in place. Remove pins.

10 Insert narrow strips of batting under each trunk and re-pin.

11 Stitch down the other side of your trunks.

12 Using gray fabric dye markers and permanent markers, shade the same sides of all your trunks.

Color lightly in a horizontal motion down the length of your trunks.

13 Apply fusible webbing to the wrong side of your leaf fabric.

14 Cut out leaves and arrange them across your tree trunks. If there are any awkward spots in your colorwash background, hide them with a cluster of leaves!

15 Fuse leaves in place, as well as any other elements you would like to add to your landscape.

16 Add borders and remove all remaining foundation.

17 Fuse the quilt top to batting, and stitch down the appliqués using monofilament thread.

18 Fuse backing to batting. Quilt as desired. Add a sleeve, hang and enjoy!

Terrace by the Sea

40½" x 53½"

Flowers highlight just about every space in this quilt –
you just can't have too many! They drip down into the
sky, they overflow their pots, and they frame the terrace
entrance. Follow the picture for fabric placement
when you are creating your colorwash backdrop.
The potted flowers are all appliquéd after the quilt
top is constructed, as are the flowers in the sky.

Fabrics

- 4 yd. 21"-22" foundation – 3 sections will be 9 squares x 10 squares and 3 sections will be 9 squares x 9 squares
- ½ yd. sky
- ⅛ yd. dark beige for the shadow on the left wall
- ⅛ yd. light beige for the light on the right side wall
- ⅛ yd. light-medium beige for the middle row of the right side wall
- ¼ yd. medium beige for both terrace walls
- ½ yd. water print
- ¼ yd. total of 2 different fabrics for flowerpots
- ¼ yd. light striped beige batik for terrace floor
- ½ yd. darker beige batik for shadows on terrace floor
- ½ yd. floral with light background (I used two different Fancy Pansy prints by Marcus Brothers)
- ½ yd. floral with dark background (should be the same version of the flowers above, only on a dark background)
- ¼ yd. green meadow for foreground hills
- ¼ yd. total of 2 light greens for meadows and distant hills
- ¼ yd. birdbath fabric
- ¼ yd. each of three different flowers for appliqué in flowerpots
- ¼ yd. small flowers and leaves to appliqué in sky
- ⅛ yd. leaf fabric for appliqué
- ⅛ yd. black fabric
- 3 birds (from a print)
- Scrap of white tulle for water in birdbath

Notions

- Monofilament thread
- Acid-free glue sticks for paper projects
- Sewing needles, size 90/14 topstitch or universal and sharps 70/10
- 6 yd. fusible webbing
- Scrap of fusible interfacing, dark
- Fabric dye markers, gray and black (optional)

A Word About Fabrics

Your lightest beige should blend with the background of the light floral. Also check the back side of one of your meadow prints; the wrong side might be just perfect at suggesting distance. The back side of one of your flowerpot fabrics might also work for another flowerpot.

Terrace pattern

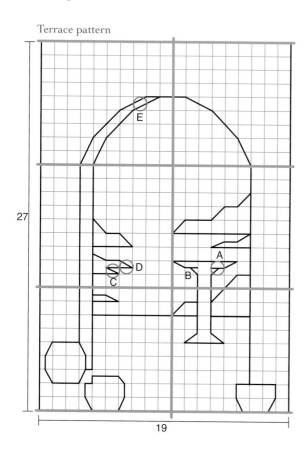

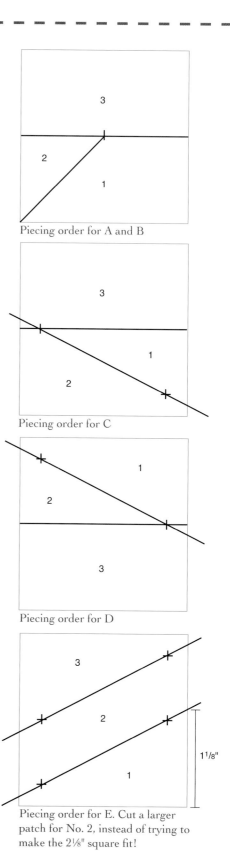

Piecing order for A and B

Piecing order for C

Piecing order for D

Piecing order for E. Cut a larger patch for No. 2, instead of trying to make the 2⅛" square fit!

Instructions

1 Draw your grid pattern on the foundation, labeling the sections and drafting careful sewing lines.

2 Cut out a 9" x 2" rectangle from your birdbath fabric, and set it aside. Cut out a 3" x ¾" piece of your dark (left) flowerpot print and set it aside. Set aside your fabrics for appliqué.

3 Cut your beiges, meadow greens, sky and water fabrics into generous 2⅛" squares. Only cut one strip or so from your light and dark background floral.

4 Begin to arrange your fabrics according to the pattern. When your arch is in place, take a careful look at your light and dark floral fabrics. You will need to blend these fabrics together.

5 For the upper-left portion of your arch, fussy-cut a few fabric squares that do not have any flowers or leaves. Arrange these squares as desired, and cut other squares with some of the dark background showing around the flowers. Add these around your dark squares. To blend into lighter areas of your arch, cut flowers from your light background florals and place them next to the flowers with the dark background. For the right side of your arch, fussy-cut areas of your light floral that are flowerless and place light flowers around these places in the same way you did with the darker side of the arch.

The flowers and leaves in the print make the connection between the light and dark backgrounds of your floral fabrics.

6 When you are satisfied with your design, follow the instructions in Chapter 3 for sewing your quilt top together. Begin sewing with your half-square triangles, rectangles and scalene triangles. Before continuing with this pattern, remove the foundation from the last set of seams only; leave the rest of the foundation on the back of your fabric squares.

7 To prepare your fabrics for appliqué, attach fusible webbing to the wrong side of the flowers and leaves, the black scrap, your flowerpot fabric and the reserved birdbath rectangle. Be sure to leave the paper on the backside of your flowerpot and birdbath print!

8 Trace the flowerpot base onto freezer paper, and press this to the prepared fabric. Cut out the shape, and fuse it to the bottom of the far-left pot. Cut out individual flowers and clumps of smaller flowers, and arrange them around your flowerpots. Arrange a hanging vine over your sky. Be sure to place enough flowers to hide the base of the arch on the right and the corner of the flowerpot on the left. Fuse in place.

9 Trace the patterns for the birdbath bowl and base on freezer paper. Cut these out, and fuse the patterns to the right side of your prepared birdbath fabric. Align the top portion of the birdbath bowl such that the narrow ends are flush with the top of the pieced birdbath. Do the same with the base of the bath. Refer to project photo if necessary.

10 Layer your white tulle in the basin of your birdbath, and stitch it in place. See Chapter 4 for more information about using tulle.

11 Fuse interfacing to the wrong side of your bird fabric and apply fusible webbing to this. Cut out birds, arrange as desired and fuse in place. Use a press cloth so as not to melt the tulle with your hot iron!

12 Cut long strips — a shy ¼" wide — from your prepared black print. Cut these into short fence pole segments, and arrange them on your quilt top. Fuse in place. Cut longer segments for rails along the top and bottom as desired.

13 Cut out elongated stipple shapes from your leftover green prints. Using your glue stick, glue them to the quilt top.

14 Sew on border fabrics. Fuse more flowers over the edge if desired.

15 Remove the rest of the foundation and fuse-baste the quilt top to the batting. Don't forget to use a press cloth to protect the tulle!

16 Stitch down all of the appliqués, including those from your fabric collage garden area. Use your sharps 70/10 needle and monofilament thread.

17 Fuse backing to batting. Bind and quilt as desired. Add a sleeve, hang and admire your handiwork!

Build a fabric collage of green prints to create a flower garden behind the birdbath.

Detail, birds and birdbath, with tulle water and garden collage.

Deepen shadows after you are finished quilting by dampening the fabric with a gray dye marker. Lightly color in some of your stipple shapes with a black marker, and blend over with the gray again.

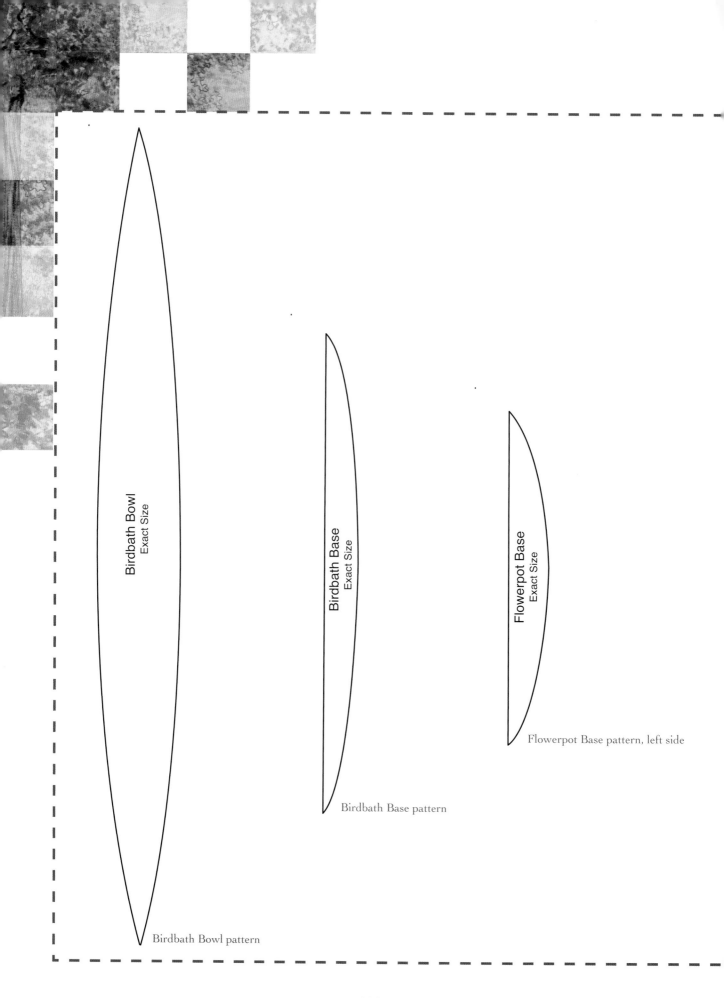

Birdbath Bowl
Exact Size

Birdbath Bowl pattern

Birdbath Base
Exact Size

Birdbath Base pattern

Flowerpot Base
Exact Size

Flowerpot Base pattern, left side

Sedona Red Rocks

37" x 30"

Here is a loose interpretation of the rock formation known as Madonna and Child. The rock striations are a result of careful placement of dark, rich red prints. The pieced border is optional; yardage is included in the fabrics list below. The inner border is an appliquéd ribbon. Follow the pattern closely; not all the rock spires are the same width.

Fabrics

- 2 yd. 21"-22" foundation – 2 sections of 9 squares x 14 squares each
- ½ yd. total of 2 foreground fabrics
- ⅛ yd. distant bluff
- ½ yd. sky blue
- ½ yd. medium sandy-red for main rock
- ⅓ yd. each of four dark-accent red prints

Notions

- 3 yd. fusible webbing
- 3 yd. black ribbon for the inner border, ¼" wide
- Sewing needles, size 90/14 topstitch or universal and sharps 70/10
- Acid-free glue sticks for paper projects
- Monofilament and fine black thread

A Word About Fabrics

Moda Marbles and Marble Mate prints make great landscape fabrics. In this quilt, they make up both the foreground and the sky! As you choose your red prints, avoid any that read as solids. Look for good combinations of texture and value in each print, and concentrate on finding a medium rock print with deeper shades in red or gray. Remember to check the back side of your fabrics. Sometimes the backs can work better than the fronts.

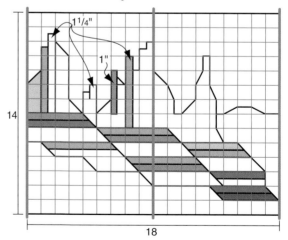

Sedona Red Rocks pattern

Instructions

1 Draft your grid and pattern onto your foundation. All unmarked rectangles are 1⅛" or half the grid square.

2 Cut your fabrics into generous 2⅛" squares. Only cut a strip or two out of each fabric, cutting more as needed. Save the remaining fabric for pieced border.

3 Arrange your squares according to the pattern. Make sure your darkest reds are placed in the long horizontal sections in the middle ground and up the left side of each rocky spire. After these are placed, blend the darkest portions of your medium red rock print into these shaded areas. Refer to the color photograph for help.

4 When you are happy with your design, follow the instructions in Chapter 3 for sewing your quilt top together. Begin sewing with your half-square and scalene triangles and rectangles. Reread page 92 if you need help piecing the tri-part squares. Before continuing with this pattern, remove the foundation from the last set of seams only; leave the rest of the foundation on the back of your fabric squares.

5 Apply fusible webbing to the wrong side of a few of your leftover rock squares.

6 Cut out lumpy spire shapes, and arrange them on the top of your rocky monuments.

Fuse rocky edge-shaped cut-outs to the pieced quilt top.

7 Fuse in place.

8 Sew on the border fabric. For pieced border, double check the paper pattern on page 112. Make sure that the finished size of each of these blocks is the same size as two of your finished squares. Adjust your pattern if necessary, and make 32 copies.

9 Paper-piece each copy.

10 Sew nine blocks together to make the top and bottom border strips. Attach to the quilt top.

11 Sew seven blocks together for each side, and sew the corner squares to finish off the border strip. Attach the borders to the quilt top.

12 Cut long ¼" strips from your fusible webbing. Peel off the paper, and lay the webbing along the seam where the border strips are attached.

13 Cut necessary lengths of ribbon, lay them on the webbing and fuse them in place.

14 Remove the rest of the foundation.

15 Fuse the quilt top to the batting and stitch down your appliqués using your sharps 70/10 needle and monofilament thread. Use black thread to stitch down the ribbon.

16 Fuse the backing to batting and quilt as desired. Bind, add a sleeve, hang and admire your handiwork!

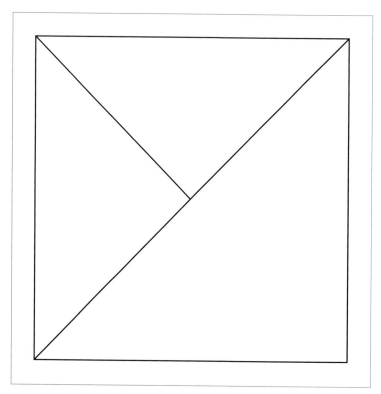

Border pattern; make 32 copies for the paper-pieced border.

A Room
with a View

30" x 36"

Here is a view through an open wrought-iron window into the Tuscan countryside. The houses are pieced, meaning you will need to draft your sewing lines carefully. The flowers in our arrangement are silk, held to the quilt top by tulle and careful stitching. The fallen petals are also captured under the layer of tulle, which adds dimension to our window box.

Fabrics

- 2 yd. 21"-22" foundation – 1 section will be 9 squares x 13 squares and the other will be 8 squares x 13 squares
- ¼ yd. blue print for vase
- ¼ yd. medium green for hillside
- ⅛ yd. medium light green for hillside
- ⅛ yd. total of 1 to 2 very light greens for distant hillside
- ¼ yd. total of 1 to 2 meadow prints for foreground
- ⅓ yd. black for wrought iron window
- ½ yd. sky
- 1¼ yd. outer border
- ⅛ yd. inner border/window trim (choose a light color to blend with outer border)
- ⅛ yd. total of 3 light beiges for houses
- ⅛ yd. total of 2 dark tans for houses
- ⅛ yd. total of 2 medium beiges for houses
- ⅛ yd. total of 4 russet-reds for rooftops
- Scraps for the following:
  Green for flower stems
  Another green for evergreen trees
  Light gray for windows
  Dark gray for doorways
- Flowers and leaves for appliqué

Notions

- Spray starch
- Sewing needles, size 90/14 topstitch or universal and sharps 70/10
- Monofilament thread
- Acid-free glue sticks for paper projects
- Freezer paper
- 3 yd. fusible webbing
- Dark red fabric marker
- ½ yd. fine tulle, dark purple
- *⅛ yd. each of two colors of tulle to layer silk flowers

  *Flowers in this wall hanging are silk. They were pulled off an arrangement and layered under a matching color of tulle. If you would rather use a cotton print, that's fine. Add ½ yd. of fusible interfacing to your notions list and fuse the interfacing to the wrong side of your large flower fabric. Instead of following the directions given for layering with tulle, just fuse your flowers in place.

A Word About Fabrics

Northcott Silk has a line of prints in sand textures. These are just great for our rooftops, stucco homes and even for our distant green hillside. Check with your local quilt shop for these fabrics.

A Room With a View pattern. See pages 118-120 for enlarged detail.

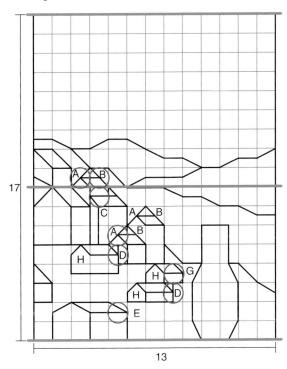

Instructions

1 Draft your grid on your foundation. Follow the patterns and dimensions very carefully to ensure that your houses will have matching rooftops!

2 Cut your fabrics into generous 2⅛" squares. Cut a 4" x 9" piece from your vase fabric and set aside. Cut your rooftop fabrics into strips, and cut off pieces as needed to piece the various rooftops.

3 Build your houses before you begin arranging your hillsides and sky. Keep the lightest homes on the edge of the village to the right and alternate your light beiges so that adjacent homes do not have the same fabric. Follow piecing order and sew the homes to the foundation.

4 Arrange your hillsides and sky, keeping your lightest greens in the distance. Place the darkest portions of your vase fabric on the right side of your vase.

5 When you are happy with your design, follow the instructions in Chapter 3 for sewing your quilt top together. Before continuing with this pattern, remove the foundation from the last set of seams only; leave the rest of the foundation on the back of your fabric squares.

6 Attach fusible webbing to the wrong side of your reserved vase fabric. Leave the paper in place.

7 Trace vase patterns to freezer paper. Cut out and compare their sizes to your pieced vase. Adjust to fit.

8 Press the freezer paper patterns to the right side of prepared vase fabric, keeping the handle, base, top rim and one side on the darkest places of your print pattern, and the middle piece on a light portion. Cut these out, and set aside the base and the bottom rim; fuse all but these pieces to your pieced vase.

9 Apply fusible webbing to the wrong side of your evergreen tree fabric, to leftover portions of your meadow prints and to window and door scraps.

10 Cut out evergreen shapes, arrange them, and fuse them in place. Cut out clumps of meadow print and fuse these to the front of some of your houses. Cut out, arrange and fuse window and door shapes.

11 Starch and press your border and black fabrics. Cut two 1¼" strips from your black fabric and sew these strips to the sides of your quilt top. Press with right sides together; open and press again.

12 Cut two 1" strips from the black, and sew these to the bottom and top of your quilt. Press as above. Trim the top and bottom strips to ⅝".

13 Cut 1" inner border strips, and 4" outer border strips. Sew these together, press open them and sew them to your quilt top, mitering your corners.

14 Attach fusible webbing to the wrong side of remaining black fabric. Cut out the following widths for your vertical window frames:

- Scant ½" x 25"
- ⅜" x 22"
- ¼" x 20"
- Scant ¼" x 18"

15 Arrange these vertical strips according to the photograph. The narrowest strip is placed on the right side of the sixth row seam. Do not fuse in place yet.

16 Cut two scant ½" x 10" strips of black print for the center horizontal window bars. Taper the width of each strip from ½" to ¼". You might want to create a freezer paper pattern for the tapered strips.

17 Cut two scant ½" x 11½" strips for the top and bottom window bars. Taper the width of each strip from ½" to ¼".

18 Arrange the horizontal strips, keeping the widest widths on the left. Trim all of the strips as needed to create a tidy frame; refer to the project photo for placement. Fuse the window frame in place.

19 Add the window latch and three small half-circle shapes for the knob and the ends of the window latch.

20 Attach fusible webbing to the back side of your green stem fabric. Cut out six to eight long, reed-shaped stems. Arrange them in the flower vase and fuse in place.

21 Fuse the base of your vase, as well the small rim, in place, covering the end of the reed-shaped stems.

22 If you are layering silk flowers under tulle, remove the remaining foundation. Press the quilt top flat. Fuse the quilt top to the batting. If you are fusing your flowers, follow the placement guidelines in the steps below, and do not remove your foundation until flowers are fused in place.

23 Arrange small flowers in spire shapes along the stems in your vase. Following the directions on page 56, layer with tulle and outline stitch using sharps 70/10 needle and monofilament thread. Cut away the excess tulle. If fusing a flower, arrange it and fuse it in place.

24 Arrange your large silk flowers. Layer, pin and outline stitch as above. Fuse larger flowers in place if you are choosing this option.

25 To create the flower centers, ball up 12"-15" of variegated green thread, and place the tangle in the center of each flower. Layer with tulle, pin and stitch in place.

26 Sprinkle some flower petals under the vase. Layer the entire bottom border strip with purple tulle. Pin tulle around the fallen petals and along the entire bottom border. Stitch along your black window frame first, then along your mitered borders and along the outside edge of the flower base. Keep tulle smoothed out as you stitch from one section to another. Outline stitch the fallen petals.

27 Layer the remaining purple tulle over the top border strip, and stitch in place as above.

28 Stitch all your appliqués in place; be sure to use sharps 70/10 needles and monofilament thread.

29 Using red fabric marker, add roof lines as necessary.

30 Fuse the backing to the batting and quilt as desired. Add a sleeve. Hang your quilt and enjoy the view!

Observe the piecing precision.

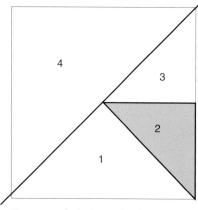

Pattern and piecing order A

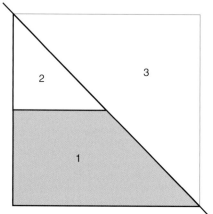

Pattern and piecing order B

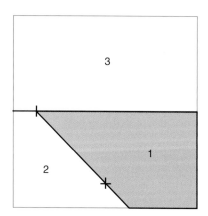

Pattern and piecing order C

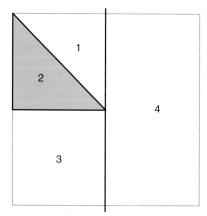

Pattern and piecing order D

NOTE: Shaded pieces represent roof fabric.

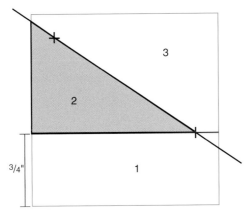

3

2

1

3/4"

Pattern and piecing order E;
reverse for F

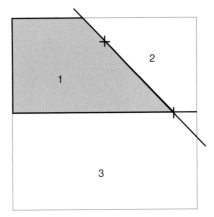

1

2

3

Pattern and piecing order G

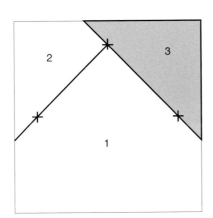

2

3

1

Pattern and piecing order H

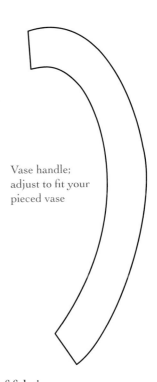

Vase handle;
adjust to fit your
pieced vase

NOTE: Shaded pieces represent roof fabric.

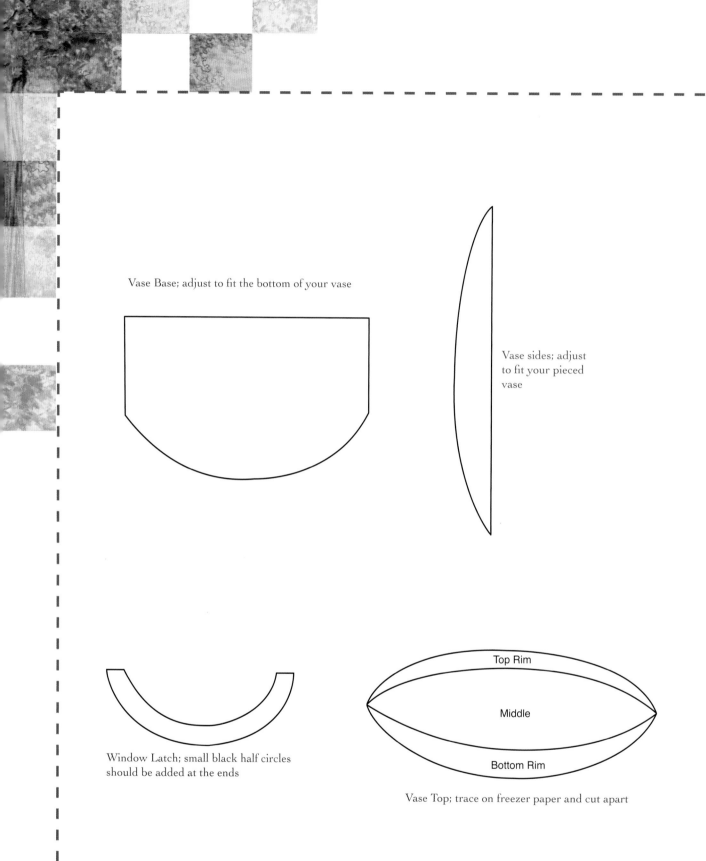

Vase Base; adjust to fit the bottom of your vase

Vase sides; adjust to fit your pieced vase

Window Latch; small black half circles should be added at the ends

Top Rim

Middle

Bottom Rim

Vase Top; trace on freezer paper and cut apart

Victorian Garden Arch

LEVEL 3

45" x 55"

Step through the arch into a time past where young girls are meandering along a garden path. Michael Miller Fabric's "Masterpiece" print recalls John Constable's paintings of rural 18ᵗʰ century England. What a perfect scene to build a dramatic Victorian garden arch around! This garden entrance pattern combines every technique I've taught you: careful drafting and sewing lines, layering with tulle, and creating bouquets with appliqué. Hang onto your hats – let's get started!

Fabrics

- 4½ yd. 21"-22" foundation — 3 sections will be 9 squares x 11 squares and 3 sections will be 9 squares x 10 squares
- 2 yd. scenic print, at least 6 repeats.
- ¼ yd. dark gray for shadow
- ¼ yd. dark brown for arch border
- ½ yd. for stone arch, should be somewhat dark
- ¼ yd. sky (should blend with the sky in scenic print)
- ½ yd. ivy foliage
- ½ yd. flower and leaf foliage for foreground plants
- ¼ yd. light cream vase print
- ½ yd. medium brown for steps
- ½ yd. light brown for steps and box front
- ⅛ yd. total of 2 light beige for flower stand. One should be very light and the other a little darker than the vase, but a little different in tone from the lightest of your steps.
- ¼ yd. red and yellow roses for appliqué (12 to 15 blossoms)
- ¼ yd. flowers and leaves for appliqué at base of arch's shadow

Notions

- 1 yd. black tulle
- Fabric dye marker, gray
- 5 yd. fusible webbing
- Sewing needles, size 90/14 topstitch or universal and sharps 70/10
- Monofilament thread
- Acid-free glue sticks for paper projects

A Word About Fabrics

The Masterpiece print has a pattern repeat that is about 24". Another scenic print of this size would also work well within our arch. If you choose to work with another scene, pick one with some height, as well as a distant, far-away look to it. Of course, any landscape scene could be created beneath our arch!

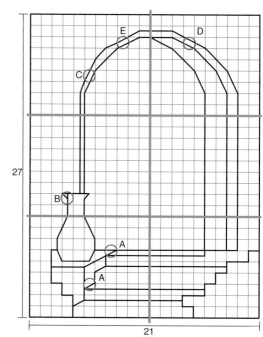

Victorian Garden Arch pattern

Instructions

1 Draft your grid and pattern on your foundation sections. All rectangles in this pattern are 1⅛".

2 Set aside all your appliqué fabrics.

3 Cut the stone arch, shadow and dark brown trim fabrics into generous 2⅛" squares. Cut some of your foreground florals and leaves, flower vase print, both browns for steps and ivy print as well. Cut more as needed.

4 Begin to design your arch. The ivy climbs up the left side and falls a bit over the top of the arch on the right. Bring in your foreground prints and start the flower vase, keeping the darkest portions of your light cream print to the left side of the vase. (I used my gray fabric dye marker to create a more shadowed look to my vase.)

5 To design your steps, use the medium and light brown prints. Save some fabric; on the narrow rectangular portion of these steps, cut these browns into shy 2⅛" strips. From these strips cut 1¾" rectangles. The back side might work especially well in creating an illusion of light shining on the top of the steps. Once the quilt top is pieced, add dark tulle to finish the shading on the bottom steps.

The flower box juts up to the stairs. The front-facing portion of the box is the same fabric as the steps. The side facing the stairs is the lightest beige and the top

should just be a tad darker than your vase.

6 Cut one repeat of your scenic print into strips. Keep the strips in order, and begin to cut squares to design the houses, keeping important parts of the design out of the seam allowances. Add more squares from other repeats to make the houses, trees and meadow larger.

The focal point in this quilt is the distant horizon; make sure you don't position it in the middle!

Use a see-through template, and fussy-cut the small figures.

7 Build the top of the steps into the scenic print by cutting into the repeat portions where the grass meets the sandy path. Arrange these grassy areas to suggest a path leading to your top step.

We will blur this area even more by cutting oval shapes out of the scenic print and fusing them to the top step. This is done after the quilt top is pieced.

8 When you are satisfied with your design, follow the instructions in Chapter 3 for sewing your quilt top together. Begin sewing with your half-square and scalene triangles and your rectangles. Remove the foundation from the last set of seams only; leave the rest of the foundation on the back of your fabric squares before continuing with this pattern.

9 Press your quilt top flat, and lay black tulle across the bottom two steps. Pin the tulle carefully, keeping everything flat. Make sure there are no loose threads trapped under the layer. (Reread Layering Tulle in Chapter 4 if necessary.)

123

11 Stitch along the top of the second step, and angle your stitching line down from the edge of the step to the bottom corners of the quilt. Make tiny stitches, and gently stitch around various flowers and leaves to create a shaded look in the garden. Cut away the excess tulle. Stitch along the bottom riser to keep the tulle in place.

12 Apply fusible webbing on the back side of your ivy print. Cut out curvy clumps to soften the line between stone and plant. Fuse in place.

13 Fuse webbing to the wrong side of your foreground flowers and leaves. Cut these out, and arrange them to create the illusion of steps rising out of the plant material. When satisfied, fuse in place.

14 Attach fusible webbing to the wrong side of the flowers and leaves you picked to hide the base of the arch on the right. Arrange and fuse in place.

15 Apply webbing to the wrong side of your red and yellow rose fabric. Cut out flowers and leaves, creating a bouquet on the surface of your quilt. Fuse in place.

16 Fuse webbing to any portion of the scenic print that you would like to be more pronounced, such as the triple-trunk birch tree. Cut out this motif, and fuse it to your landscape. Cut and fuse oval-shaped portions of scenic print to blend the path into the stairs. If you have any problem spots, hide them by cutting and fusing parts of the scenic print on top.

17 Sew on your border strips. Be careful with your hot iron and your tulle!

18 Remove the remaining foundation. Be careful not to rip out any of your stitches, and don't worry about getting every bit off.

Layer the bottom two steps and risers with black tulle, angling the stitching down into the foreground flowers.

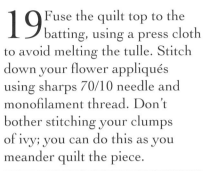

19 Fuse the quilt top to the batting, using a press cloth to avoid melting the tulle. Stitch down your flower appliqués using sharps 70/10 needle and monofilament thread. Don't bother stitching your clumps of ivy; you can do this as you meander quilt the piece.

20 Fuse the backing to the batting and quilt as desired. Bind, add a sleeve, hang and enjoy your masterpiece!

Build a beautiful rose bouquet and shade the bottom of your flower pot with a gray marker.

Vase Bottom

Vase Bottom pattern

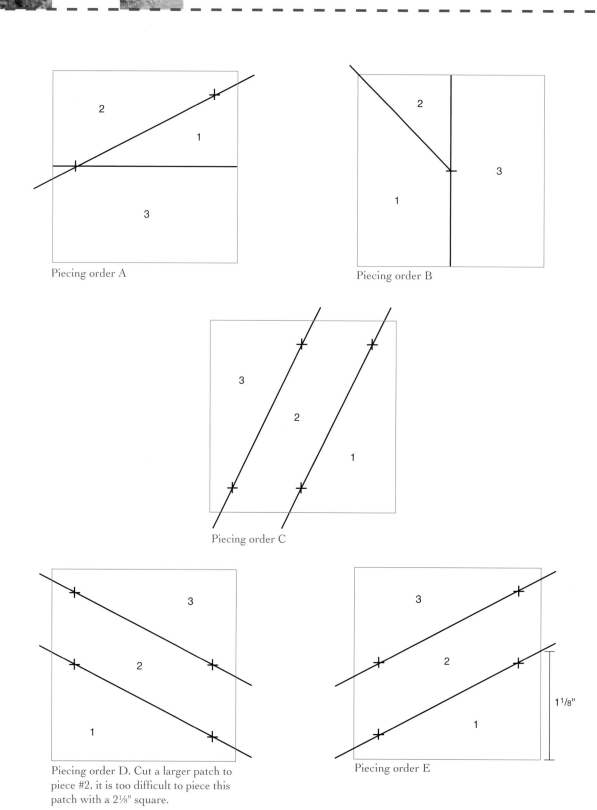

Piecing order A

Piecing order B

Piecing order C

Piecing order D. Cut a larger patch to piece #2, it is too difficult to piece this patch with a 2⅛" square.

Piecing order E

1⅛"

Resources

The Internet has opened a door to visual feasts from some of the finest photographers in the world. Their galleries are filled with photos of some of the most beautiful places on earth. From color combinations to the angle from which the scene is shot, there is plenty to be learned by studying the works of other landscape artists. Here are a few of my favorites:

www.jamesrandklev.com
www.larrycarver.com
www.donnelly-austin.com
www.terragalleria.com

Fabrics

United Notions / Moda Fabrics
www.modafabrics.com
13800 Hutton Drive
Dallas, TX 75234
Phone: 800-527-9447
- Moda Marbles
- Marble Mates

Northcott Silk
www.northcott.net
1099 Wall St. W.
Lyndhurst, NJ 07071
Phone: 201-672-9600

Troy Corporation
www.troy-corp.com
2701 N. Normandy Ave.
Chicago, IL 60707-3605
Phone: 800-888-2400
- Johanna Wilson — River Woods, Hickory Mountain

Marcus Brothers
www.marcusbrothers.com
980 Ave. of the Americas
New York, NY 10018
Phone: 212-354-8700
- Mary Mulari – Lake Superior Collection
- Natalie Sewell – A Walk in the Woods
- Faye Burgos – Fancy Pansy, Pansy Potpourri

Michael Miller Fabrics
www.michaelmillerfabrics.com
118 W. 22nd St., Fifth Floor
New York, NY 10011
Phone: 212-704-0774

Stabilizers

Hammer Brothers
407 Grand Blvd.
Kansas City, MO 64106
Phone: 800-321-2351
Email: info@sewstable.com
(F-810, 1 oz. lightweight tear-away – 21" width)

Handler Textile Corporation (HTC)
24 Empire Blvd.
Moonachie, NJ 07074
(HTC Tear-Away, Rinse-Away, and Fundation all at 22" width)

Pellon – Wonder Under
Web site: www.shopellon.com
Widely available at sewing and quilt shops, I strongly recommend this product for projects in this book.

Internet Fabric Shops

www.bighornquilts.com
www.virginiaquilter.com
www.craftconn.com
www.equilter.com
www.quiltshops.com
www.quiltfabriconline.com

Books

"Simple Thread Painting" by Nancy Prince

"Guide to Machine Quilting" by Diane Gaudynski

Krause Publications
www.krause.com
Phone: 888-457-2873

Other Resources

Annie's Attic
www.anniesattic.com
1 Annie Lane
Big Sandy, TX 75755
Phone: 800-582-6643

Keepsake Quilting
www.keepsakequilting.com
Route 25
P.O. Box 1618
Center Harbor, NH 03226-1618
Phone: 800-438-5464

About the Author

Cathy Geier has a bachelor of arts degree from the University of Wisconsin-Madison in Art History; she specifically studied 19th century landscapes in English and French art. Many of her quilts have been juried into national shows. Cathy enjoys lecturing and teaching her landscape quilt methods both regionally and nationally. She is married with three almost-grown children, and her husband's job with the Forest Service has led her family to some of the most scenic places in the country. Her quilts reflect her love of the forests, mountains and lakes around her.